Crafts for Kids

3rd Edition

99 Fun Packed Projects for Kids of All Ages

by Kitty Moore

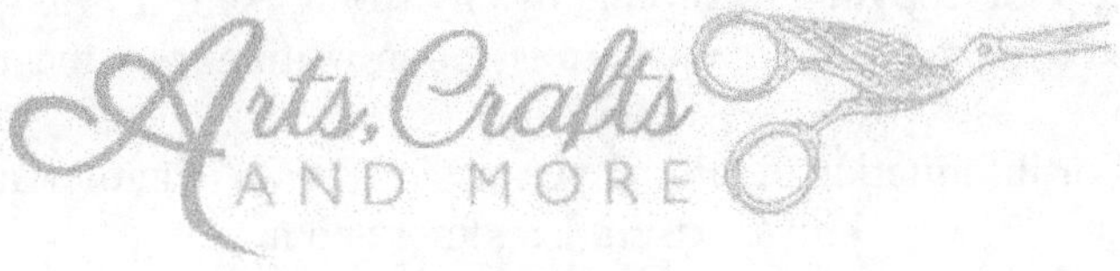

Kitty Moore
ArtsCraftsAndMore.com

Table of Contents

Introduction

These 99 fun packed projects for kids of all ages will enchant, challenge, and inspire you and your children.

Every project can be easily adapted to any child's level, as these brilliant ideas and crafts can be made as simple or as intricate as you want!

The simple instructions come with lists of all the materials you'll need to make dazzling sun catchers, portable pop-up houses, wax paper wonders, party piñatas, and much, much more!

1. Portable Pop-Up Doll House

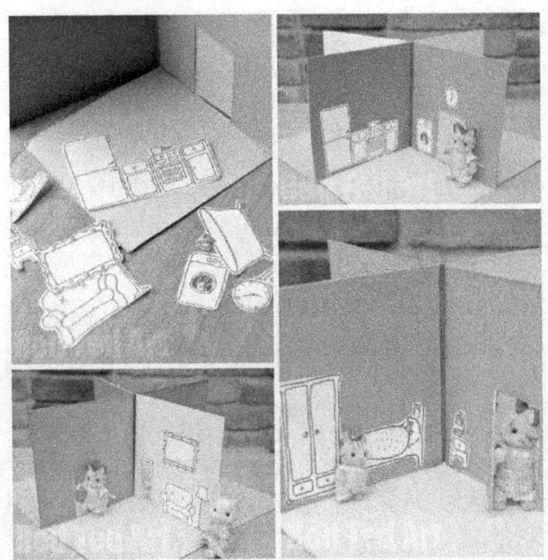

Materials

- Two empty cereal boxes
- Strong adhesive tape
- Colored paper/paint
- White paper
- Pens

- Ruler
- Scissors
- Glue stick
- Pencil
- Old magazines

Directions

1. Unfold the cereal boxes and neatly cut out the main panels so you have four. Fold each panel in half and measure a square on each side of the crease. Draw the lines, cut along them and repeat with the three other panels.

2. Take two panels, and lay them side-by-side. One should have the printed side facing up, and the other should have the plain side up. Tape the top half of the two pieces together on both sides of the joint. Use several layers of tape or strong duct tape to make them more durable.

3. Fold the right panel on top of the left, and place the third panel beside it. Tape that in place as before (half-way up) and repeat with the fourth panel. Now that all the panels are joined you can open it up and create a 3D, four-room layout. When you fold it back up, it makes a tidy little book. Now that you have the house, it's time to decorate!

4. First, you need doors to get into the rooms. Choose where you want them and mark them with a pencil. A good tip is to measure the doors based on the toys that will "live" in the house. Make sure they fit! Unfold the house, lay it flat, and use a craft knife to make three slices for the door. (Don't worry if you forget about the hinges. If you slice four and the door falls out, just use tape to secure it.)

5. For the walls, cut pieces of colored paper to size and use the glue stick and press in place. Or paint them. Do the same for the floors. Cut pictures from magazines for wall clocks, dressers, TVs, and anything else you want. Use the glue stick

to glue them in place. Be as minimal or over-the-top as you want!

2. Finger Painted Hyacinth Blossoms

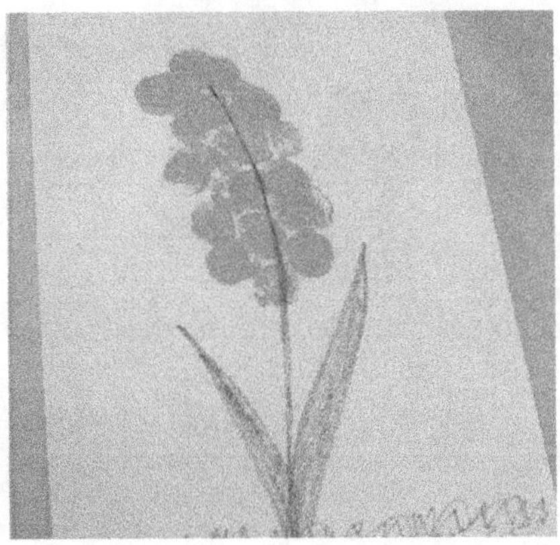

Materials

- Crayons and markers
- Paper
- Finger paint

Directions

1. Use the markers and crayons to draw the leaves and grass at the bottom of the page. Draw two long stems in a darker color rising up the page.

2. Paint the petals using only one finger, dabbing along both sides of the stems. Repeat with a second color.

3. When the paint is dry, use a black crayon to outline the petals. Now you can paint in the sky or background. Your hyacinth is finished!

3. Easy 'Stained' Glass Windows

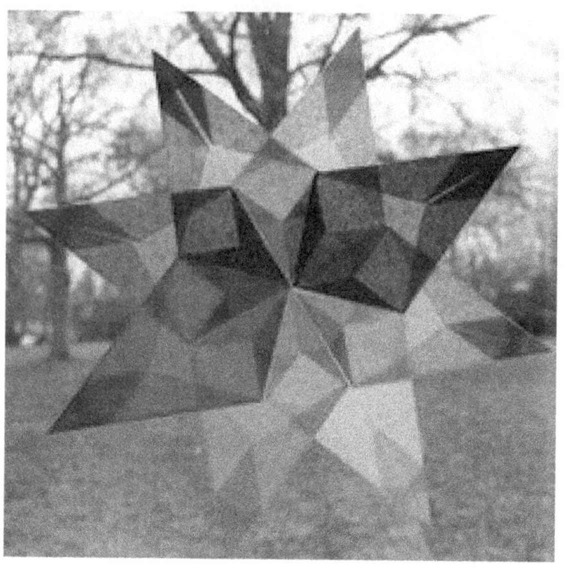

Materials

- Colored cellophane paper
- Scissors
- Dish soap and water

Directions

1. Cut the cellophane into small circles, triangles, squares, or whatever shapes you want. Mix one part of water to two parts dish soap. This will be your glue.

2. Use your fingers or a brush to apply the soap solution to the window and stick on your shapes.

3. Arrange the shapes in a pattern or just put them anywhere. Now enjoy your beautiful stained-glass window!

4. Blossoming Branches

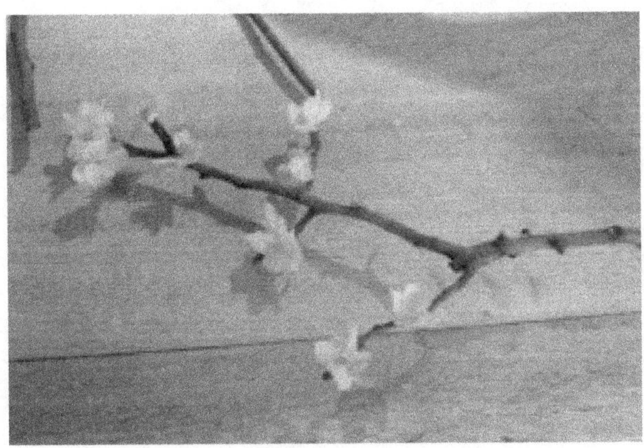

Materials

- Colored cardstock
- Scissors
- Clear craft glue
- Branch

Directions

1. Cut the cardstock into 5" squares. Fold in half, and fold in half again. Open the square and crease diagonally one way and then the other.

2. Refold the square and cut a heart shape along the open edges. Don't cut too close to the center.

3. Use another color of cardstock to cut out leaves. Attach the flowers and leaves to a branch using clear craft glue.

I have included a bonus just for you…

FOR A LIMITED TIME ONLY – Get my best-selling book "DIY Crafts: The 100 Most Popular Crafts & Projects That Make Your Life Easier" absolutely FREE!

Readers who have downloaded the bonus book as well have seen the greatest changes in their crafting abilities and have expanded their repertoire of crafts – so it is *highly recommended* to get this bonus book today!

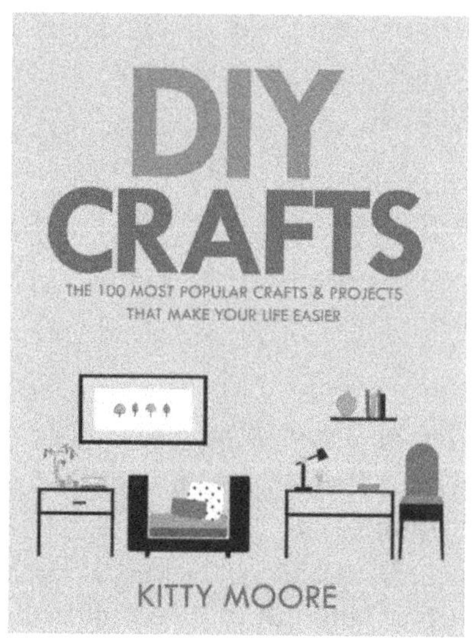

Get your free copy at:

ArtsCraftsAndMore.com/Bonus

5. Personalized Painted Mugs

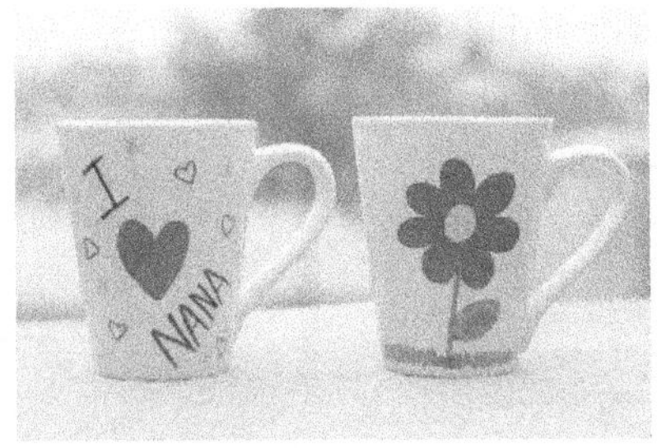

Materials

- Ceramic paint pen
- Mug
- Oven

Directions

1. Draw your design or write your message on the mug with the ceramic paint pen. The design can be as simple or intricate as you want.

2. Let the paint dry for 24 hours before baking the mugs to make the paint dishwasher safe. Have an adult bake the mug at 300 degrees Fahrenheit for 30 minutes.

6. Beautiful Bunting

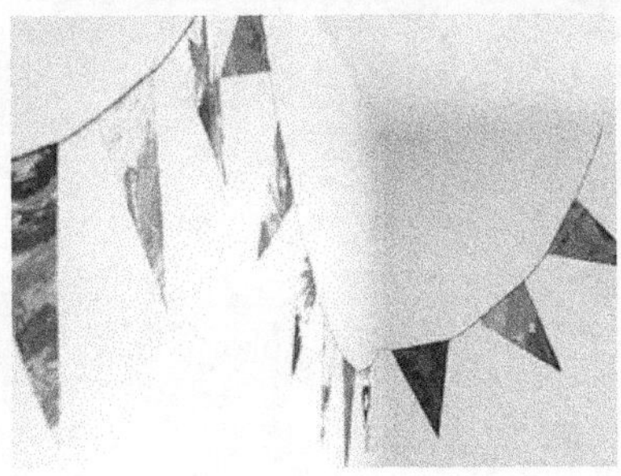

Materials

- White and colored paper
- Paint and brushes (optional)
- Scissors
- String
- Tape

Directions

1. Choose your paper and cut it into large triangles. You can use any colored or decorative paper you want. You could even use your child's artwork or paint new designs.

2. Use tape to attach the triangles to the string. The easiest way is to make a small fold along the base of the triangle and slip the string under it. Tie the string and hang it in your home. Don't be restricted to triangles; experiment with other shapes and cut leaves, flowers, clouds, or whatever you like!

7. Confetti Tape

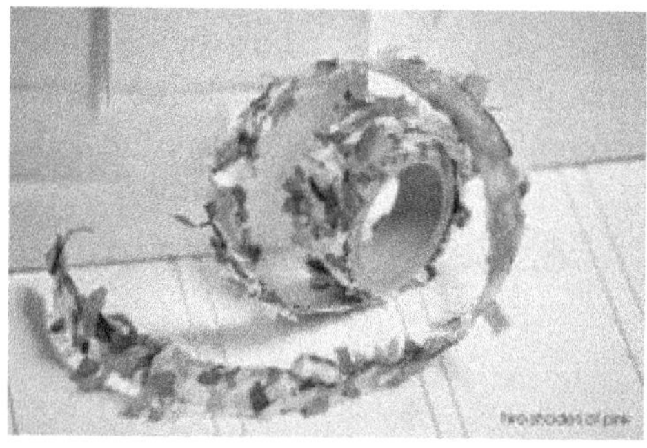

Materials

- Tissue paper
- Scissors
- Double sided tape

Directions

1. Make your own confetti by cutting the tissue paper into tiny bits with the scissors.

2. Make a thick line with the colorful bits or paper on the table, and unroll a length of double-sided tape.

3. Start dabbing one side of the tape on the paper to pick up the confetti. Make sure to leave the other side of the tape clean. You can use your confetti tape to decorate edges of other projects or to fasten gifts or lunch bags!

8. Finger Print Key Rings

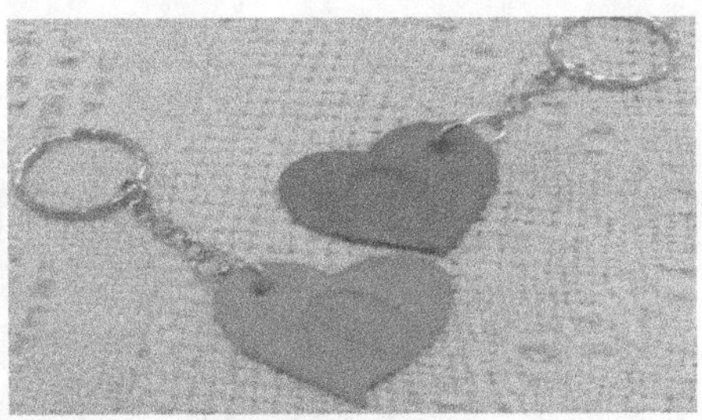

Materials

- Oven bake clay
- Key chain rings and small jewelry rings
- Metallic paint and brushes
- Cookie cutter
- Oven

Directions

1. Roll out the clay like you would dough. Choose your cookie cutter, and cut out your shapes. Press your fingers into the clay. Poke a small hole into the top of each (for the ring fitting).

2. Bake the clay following the instructions on the packaging, and wait for them to cool. Brush on the metallic paint to completely cover the baked clay. It may take more than one coat.

3. Put a small jewelry ring through the hole and then feed this through the larger key ring chain. You can bling them up a bit more by adding small 'jewels' to the jewelry ring if you wish.

9. Sweet Dreams Personalized Pillow Case

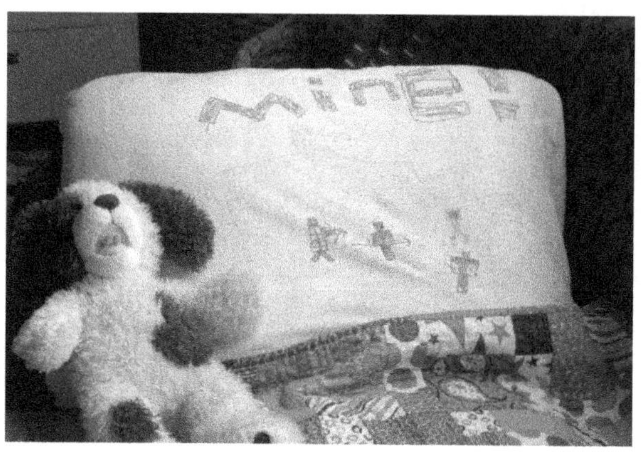

Materials

- Plain white pillowcase
- Pencil and paper
- Fabric markers
- Length of cardboard
- Clothes iron

Directions

1. Put the cardboard inside the pillowcase, and pull it tight. (The cardboard stops the ink from soaking through and makes the pillowcase easier to write on).

2. Choose your personal message, and write it on the paper. "I Love You" is always a good option! Use the pencil to first write the message on the pillowcase and don't worry about any mistakes.

3. Go over the message with the fabric markers and add any extra touches or flourishes you want. Make the marks permanent by ironing the pillowcase, and then wash it to remove any unwanted pencil marks.

10. Put Your Art on Candles

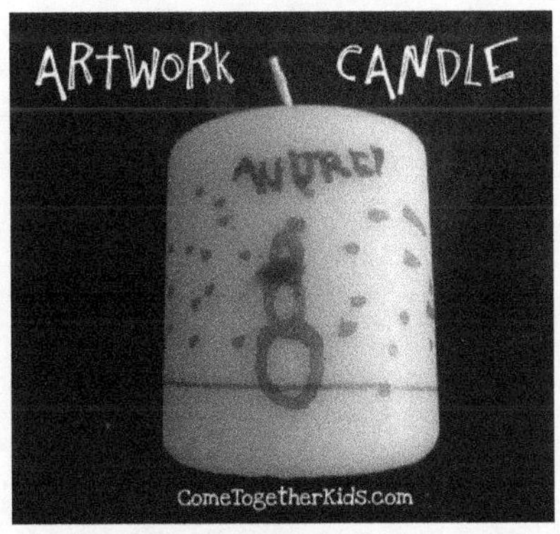

Materials

- White tissue paper
- Markers
- Scissors
- White pillar candles
- Parchment or waxed paper
- Hair dryer

Directions

1. Wrap the candle with the tissue paper and cut it to fit. Remove the tissue paper. Using the markers, draw your designs. Tissue paper is delicate, so be careful. Rewrap the

candle with the artwork and then wrap that with your waxed paper or parchment paper.

2. Now use the hairdryer to transfer the design onto the candle. Turn the hair dryer to high heat, and hold it close to the candle. The tissue paper will slowly disappear. When it is no longer visible, you can stop. Carefully unwrap the waxed paper to reveal the art candle. This makes a beautiful gift for anyone!

11. Sugar Scrub Pampering Set

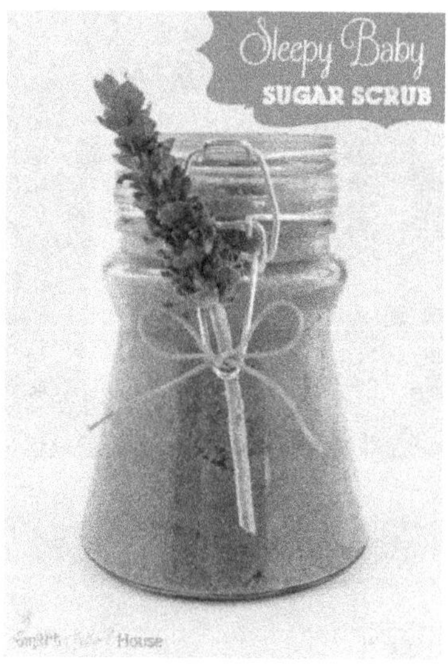

Materials

- 3 cups of white sugar
- 1 cup and 2 tablespoons olive oil
- Essential oils (lavender, jasmine, vanilla, etc.)
- Food coloring (optional)
- Mixing bowl
- Jar with a top
- Ribbon

Directions

1. Mix together the sugar, olive oil, and about 10 drops of essential oils. If you're using food coloring, add a few drops. Make sure to not add too much. You don't want to end up dying your skin!

2. When the ingredients have been well mixed, pack the sugar scrub into your jar. Add a special touch by tying the ribbon around it or add a personalized sticker.

12. Bath Bomb!

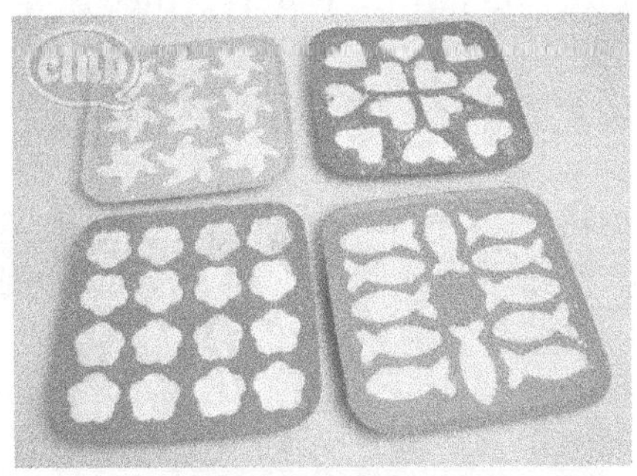

Materials

- 2 cups of bicarbonate/baking soda
- 1-2 tablespoons of olive oil
- Food coloring
- 1 cup cream of tartar
- Water in a spray bottle
- Silicone ice cube tray

Directions

1. Mix all the ingredients well until you are happy with the color.

2. Give it 2-3 sprays of water and start mixing until it feels a bit like wet sand (the water will make the baking soda fizz). When you can make a good indent and shape with a spoon without it crumbling, the mix is ready.

3. Transfer it into the silicone ice cube trays (other trays work but it's very hard to remove your 'bombs' without them breaking).

4. Press the mix down hard and let them dry and harden for one or two days.When they are set, gently remove the 'bombs' and put them into nice bags. If they break apart when you remove them from the tray, don't panic. Simply crumble it all up again, spray on a little water, remix it, and try again.

13. Key Wind Chime

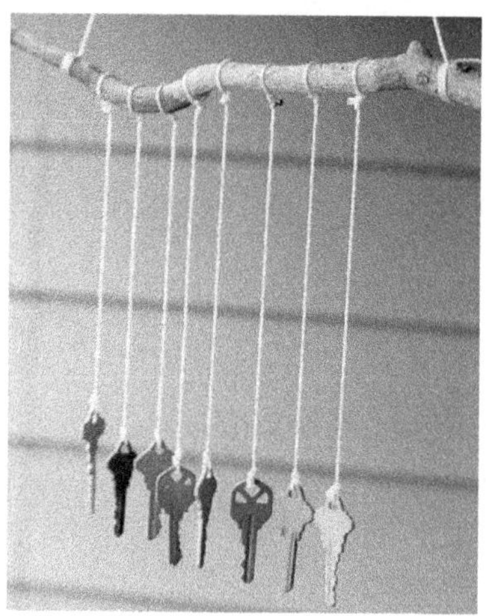

Materials

- 5 or more old keys
- Stick or branch
- String or fishing line
- Acrylic paint

Directions

1. Paint the keys and stick carefully. You might need a couple of coats to get a good finish. Tie the string to each end of the stick and hang it.

2. Tie a length of string to each key, and then tie them all to the stick. Make sure they are close enough to chime when the wind blows.

14. Eggshell Seed Bombs

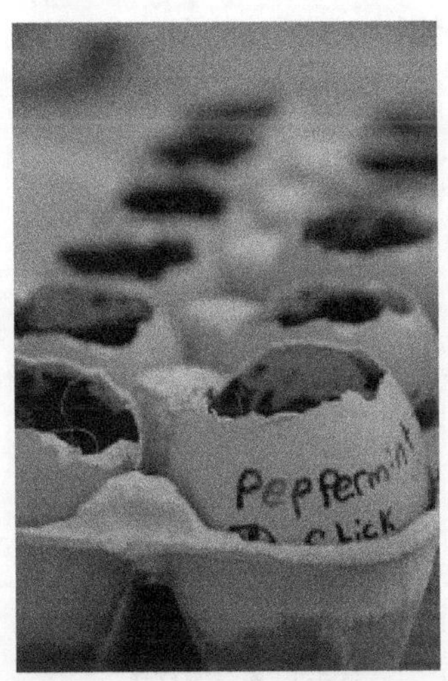

Materials

- Blown and dried eggshells
- Drill with two bits
- Flower seeds
- Soil/compost
- Small funnel
- Glue
- Paint brush
- Tissue paper

Directions

1. Carefully drill a small hole at the top of the egg and a slightly larger one at the bottom. Blow the yolk and egg white out. Ensure the shells are dry and handle them carefully.

2. Glue a little bit of tissue paper over the small hole. Allow it to dry, and then insert your funnel into the larger one. Mix the flower seeds with the compost or soil, and gently fill the eggs (you don't need to fill them completely).

3. Seal the hole with tissue paper and glue and paint the eggs. They make brilliant Easter gifts for grandparents and friends, or you can throw them in your own garden!

15. My Crafty Canvas Bag

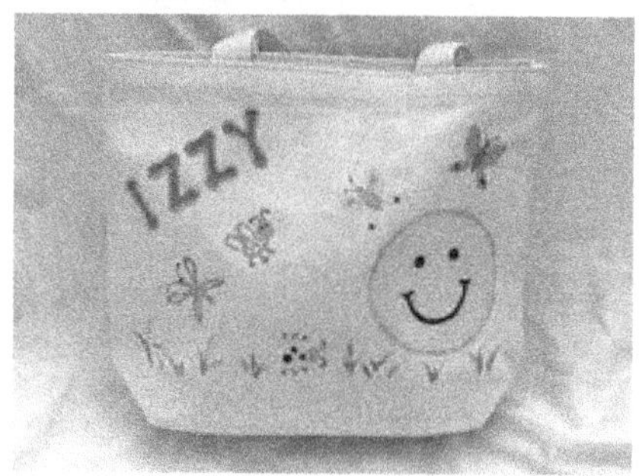

Materials

- Plain canvas bag (available at craft stores)
- Fabric paint (acrylic will also work)
- Clothes iron
- Sponge
- Scissors
- Pencil
- Freezer paper (for stencil)
- Cardboard

Directions

1. Choose the design you want for your bag. Get inspiration from easy images or a simple phrase. Place a sheet of freezer paper (with the plastic side down) over the design and trace over it. Cut the design out of the freezer paper to create your stencil.

2. Place it in position on your bag, with the plastic side down and iron it carefully onto the bag. Insert the cardboard into the bag to stop the paint bleeding through to the other side and then start sponging the paint over the stencil.

3. Wait five or ten minutes to allow the paint to dry a little, and then carefully peel off the stencil. You can use fabric markers to add any finishing touches or paint on extra designs.

16. Pirate Cork Boats

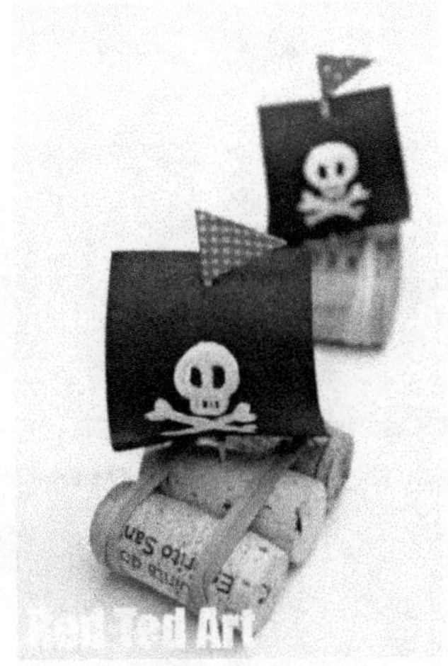

Materials

- 3 corks (from wine bottles)
- Toothpick
- Black paper, cardstock, or craft foam

- White paint
- 2 elastic bands
- String (optional)
- Scissors
- Glue

Directions

1. Put the 3 corks side by side and glue them together before putting the elastic bands around them.

2. Make the sail by cutting the black paper, cardstock, or craft foam into a small rectangle, and paint on the skull and cross bones.

3. Pierce the sail with the toothpick at the top and bottom, creating a slight bend. Poke the toothpick into the middle of the center cork. You're ready to set sail!

17. Pop-Art Masterpiece

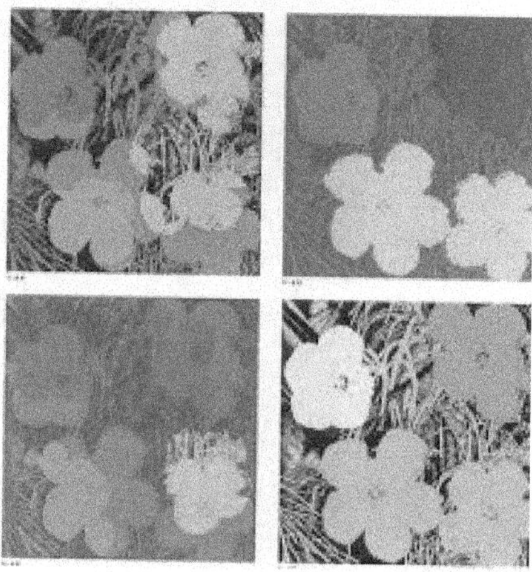

Materials

- Watercolor paper

- Acrylic paints and large tub (big foil baking trays are ideal)
- Watercolor paint
- Painter's tape
- Glossy cardstock
- Brushes and cups for water
- Pencil and scissors

Directions

1. Draw large flower shapes on the glossy cardstock and cut around them. Pour the acrylic paint into the tub and place the flower heads, glossy side down, into the paint.

2. Next put the flower heads paint side down onto the watercolor paper. Lift the flowers off and allow the paint to dry. While waiting, use the painter's tape to start cutting shapes mimicking blades of grass.

3. Place these around the flowers in a scattered pattern. Use watercolor paint to cover the space around the flowers and over the tape. Peel off the tape and then paint in the 'grass'.

18. Homemade Play Dough

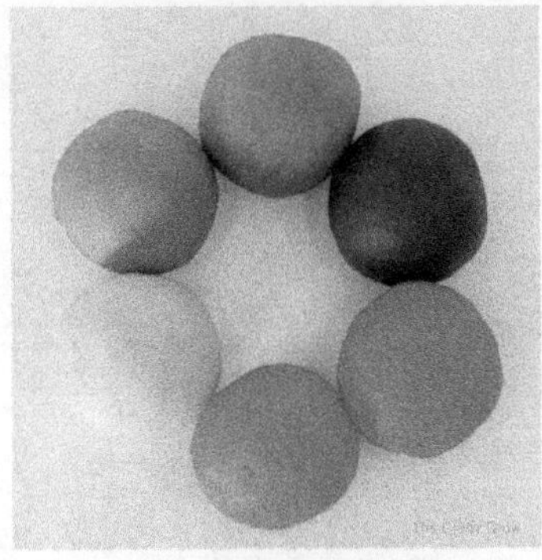

Materials

- ½ cup flour

- ½ cup water
- 2 tbsp salt
- Food color
- 1 tsp cream of tartar
- Non-stick saucepan and stove
- Parchment paper

Directions

1. Mix the flour, water, salt, and cream of tartar in the saucepan making sure you get a nice smooth consistency. Next, add the food coloring and mix it thoroughly. Put the pan on the stove and heat slowly, stirring frequently.

2. As the mix thickens, stir constantly. It will start to pull away from the sides of the pan after about 5 minutes. Remove from the heat; put the dough ball on some parchment paper to cool.

3. Knead the dough for a minute or so. Now you're ready to go! You can store it by wrapping it in parchment paper and keeping it inside a plastic zipper bag.

19. Potato Print Gift Paper

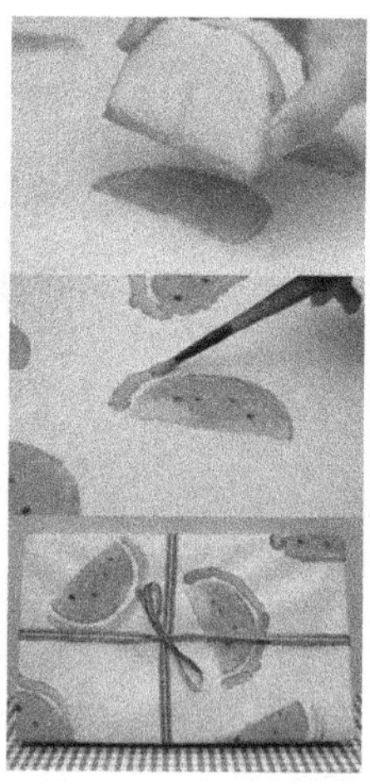

Materials

- Newspaper
- Potato
- Cookie cutter
- Knife
- Paper towel
- Paint and brush

Directions

1. Push in the cookie cutter into the potato, and cut around it with the knife. Remove the cutter and slice across the potato to make a flat surface. Dry the potato on the paper towel before painting it with a brush. Apply the paint to the newspaper by pushing the potato down. Reapply paint as necessary.

2. Move the potato diagonally to create a pattern, or make a random design using different colors for contrast. Allow each sheet to dry and then get ready to wrap!

20. Floating Angel

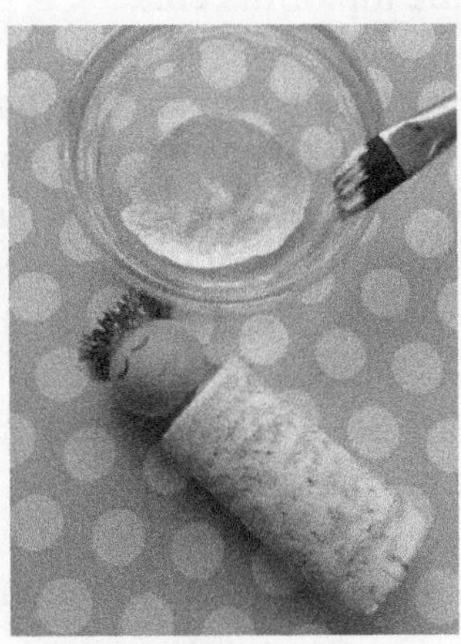

Materials

- Cork from a wine bottle
- Pink paint
- Paintbrush
- Tin foil
- Paper
- Wool
- Ribbon
- Glue and tape
- Markers

Directions

1. Paint the cork pink. Cut a semi-circle out of white paper (trace around a cup for the shape) and fit it around the cork creating a flute like effect for the dress.

2. Leave the top third of the cork visible and secure the dress to the cork using tape or glue.

3. Cut strands of wool for the angel's hair and make a little halo by rolling up some tin foil and forming a circle. Glue the hair and halo onto the top of the cork.

4. Make a small rectangle from white paper. Fold and cut out the shape of a wing. Open the paper and you will have a pair of wings. Glue some tin foil to both sides of the wings, and then glue them onto the back of the angel.

5. Add a ribbon loop between the wings as a hanger. You can cut a small heart out of the foil and glue it onto the angel's front for a nice little extra touch.

6. Add facial features by drawing them on with the markers.

21. Wax Paper Wonder

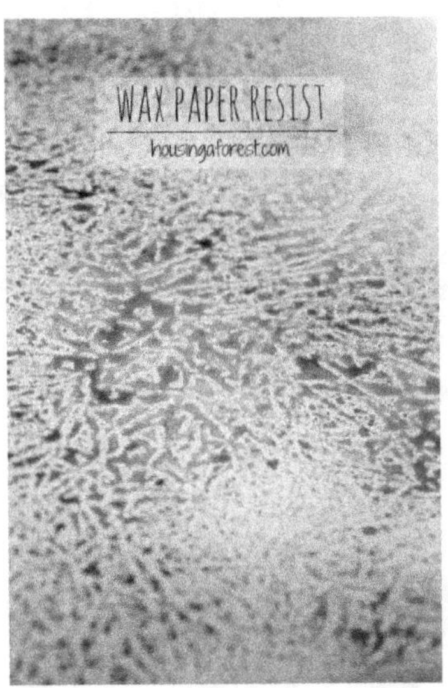

Materials

- Wax paper
- Plain paper
- Spray bottles with water tinted with food coloring
- Clothes iron

Directions

1. Crumple some sheets of wax paper into a ball or make lots of regular folds. Sandwich the crumpled wax paper between two sheets of plain paper. Iron the paper slowly back and forth. Make sure it's dry and don't use steam. The wax will transfer in patterns onto the plain paper.

2. Peel away the plain paper and use the side that has the wax on it. Get prepared to be mesmerized when you start spraying the colored water onto the paper. (This could get messy, so use the sink or cover workspace first!)

22. Super Self-Powered Tug Boat

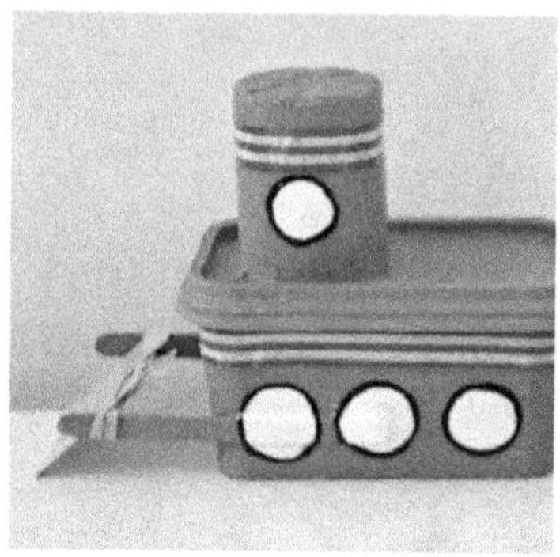

Materials

- Empty margarine tub and extra lid
- Empty yogurt cup
- Duct tape
- Acrylic paint
- 2 flat craft sticks
- Elastic band

Directions

1. Tape the craft sticks to both sides of the tub. Secure the upturned yogurt cup at one end of the lid with duct tape.

2. Paint the tub, pot, craft sticks, and your extra lid with acrylic paint. When they are dry you can add some features by painting on windows or deck features. Or you could use colored tape to add trim around the boat.

3. Cut a small rectangle (slightly smaller than the width of the boat) out of the extra lid to make the paddle. Put a hole at both sides and feed it through the elastic band. Attach the bands to the sticks, wind up, and let the boat go!

23. Unsinkable Snowman

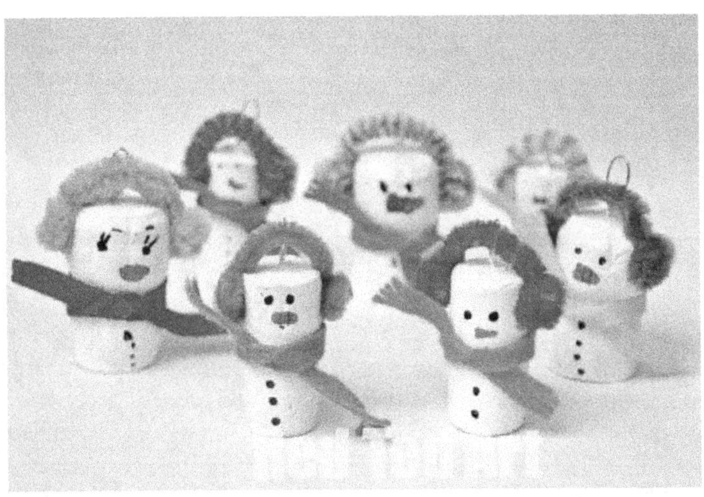

Materials

- Champagne cork
- White acrylic paint and brush
- Pipe cleaners or twigs
- Wool
- Black and orange markers
- Scissors

Directions

1. Paint the cork white. Make a hole in the thin end of the cork with the tip of the scissors.

2. Push in some wool for hair. Make holes in the sides of the cork and push in the pipe cleaners or twigs for the arms.

3. Finally, draw on the face. Use the markers to make a "carrot" nose, eyes, and mouth, and dab on the buttons.

24. Non-Slip Mouse Pad

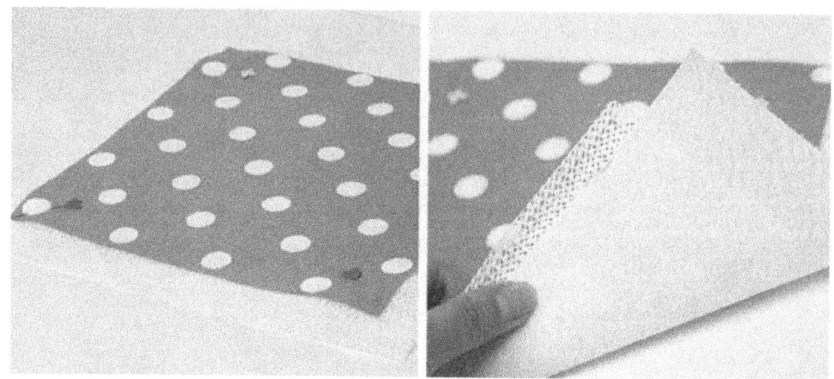

Materials

- Cardboard (6" x 8")
- Fabric (8" x 10")
- Craft foam (2 sheets, 6" x 8")
- Hot glue and gun
- Scissors

Directions

1. Cut the cardboard to whatever shape you want (rectangles are the easiest to cover with fabric). Glue the craft foam to the cardboard.

2. Position your fabric and lay down a line of hot glue all the way around the edge of the foam. Pull the fabric tight and tidy the corners with extra glue.

3. Take the second sheet of craft foam and trim it to just slightly smaller than the mouse pad. Cover with hot glue and press the foam in place. Your non-slip mouse pad will be ready for use when the glue has dried (just a few minutes).

25. Slime in No Time!

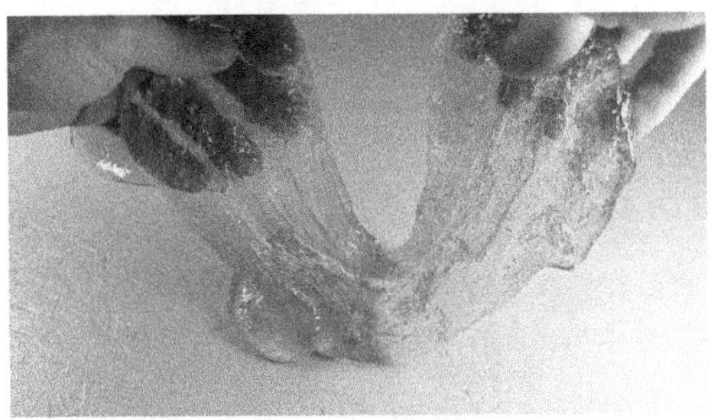

Materials

- 1 cup of corn flour
- 1 cup of water
- Food coloring (optional)

Directions

1. Put the corn flour and food color into a bowl, and gradually
   add the water as you mix. Your slime will appear slimy one
   minute, and then solid the next! Add more corn flour or water
   as necessary. That's it. Enjoy!

26. Stepping Stone Fun

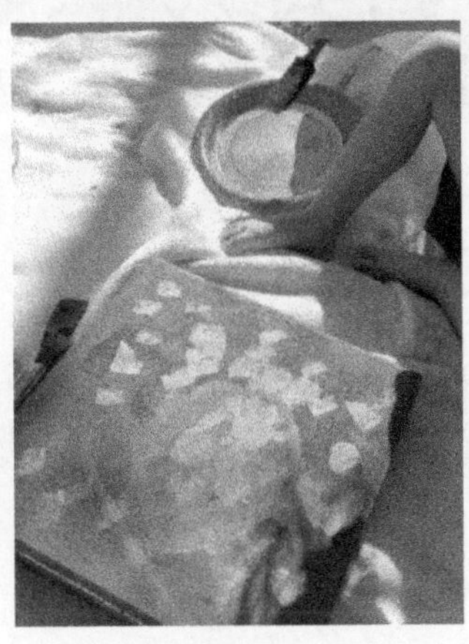

Materials

- Flagstones
- Painter's tape
- Masonry paint
- Brushes or sponges

Directions

1. Make sure the flagstones are clean, dry, and free of dust. Use the painter's tape to mask off a design, number, word, or pattern.

2. Apply the paint with brushes or sponges in any pattern you wish. Remove the tape, allow the stones to dry, and then place in your yard or garden for stepping stone fun.

27. Party Piñata

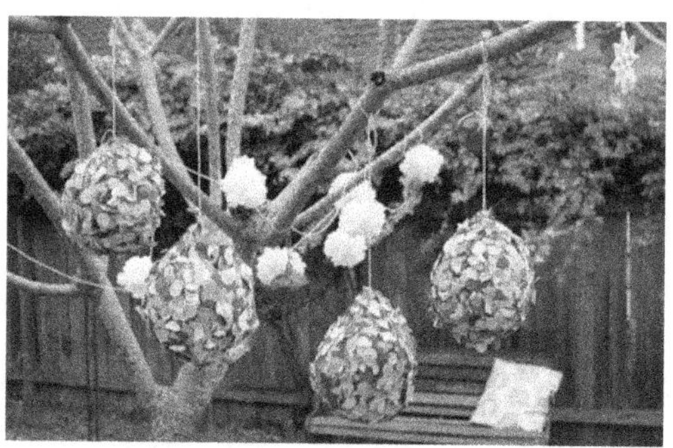

Materials

- Big balloon
- Newspapers torn into strips
- White paper towels
- White glue
- Paint and brushes
- Painter's tape
- Egg carton

- Wire
- Mix of candy
- String for hanging
- Stick

Directions

1. Blow up the balloon, and mix your paper mâché paste (approximately half white glue and half water). Mix well and begin dipping newspaper strips, one at a time, into the glue. Stick the strips to the balloon.

2. After two layers of newspaper strips are added, use the egg carton to glue bumps on and then cover these with two more layers of paper mâché. Use strips of the white paper towels for the final layer. Allow the paper to dry completely. This can take a few days.

3. When it is dry, cut out a small hole near a bump that's big enough to put the candy in before closing the hole with glue and paper. Decorate with paint and allow it to dry. Poke two holes near the top and thread through some string, Tie in a loop and use this to help hang the candy filled piñata.

28. Colorful Ice Tower

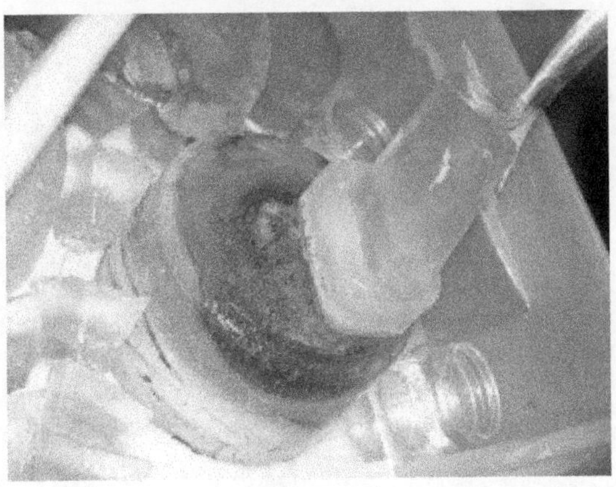

Materials

- Plastic containers in various sizes
- Ice cube trays
- Water and food coloring
- Freezer
- Bowl for hot water (big enough for your largest container)
- Gloves (optional)

Directions

1. Mix various food colors with water and fill your containers. The more varied sizes and shapes, the better. Put the containers in a freezer, or, if it's winter and cold enough, leave them outside overnight. Use a bowl of hot water and dip the containers in them to release the ice. Start stacking them into a tower or whatever structure you like.

2. Hold each one in place for a few moments. You may want to slip on your gloves. The dripping water will refreeze, forming a bond that sticks them together. Keep in mind that ice melts and food color can stain, so build your tower away from your decking or paving.

29. Rustic Photo Frame

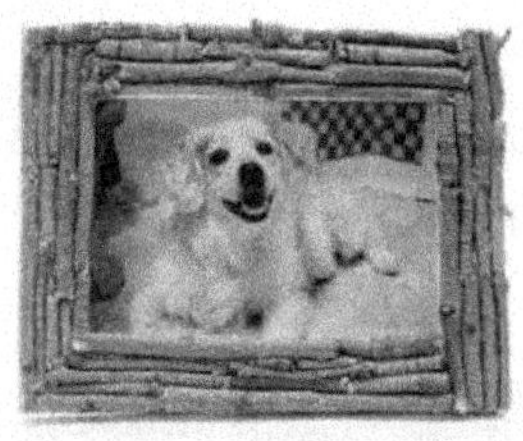
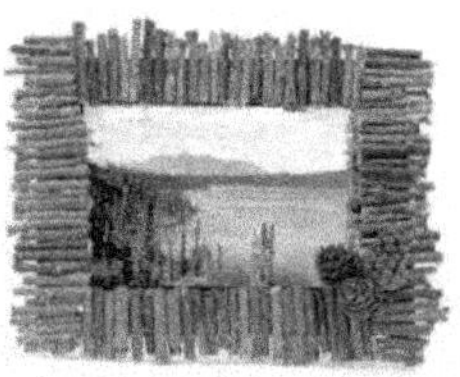

Materials

- Twigs
- Wood frame
- Hot glue and gun

Directions

1. Gather your twigs and measure them to fit the frame's border, and then break them to size. You can arrange them vertically, horizontally, or diagonally.

2. Apply hot glue to the frame, and attach the twigs. Continue until the whole frame is covered. This makes a wonderful gift, or you can keep it for yourself!

30. Groundhog Day Mask

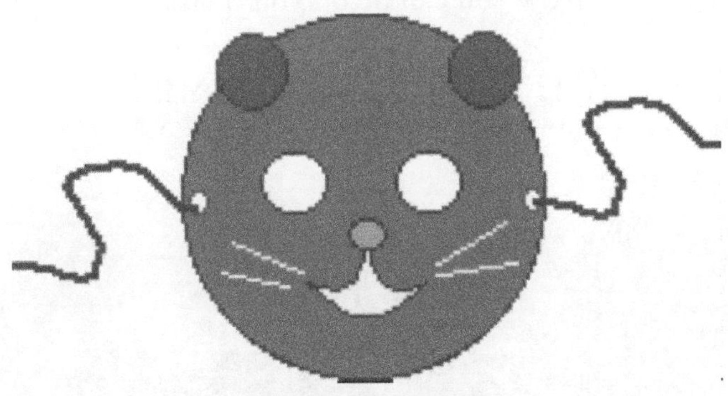

Materials

- Paper plate
- Brown paint and paintbrush
- Brown construction paper
- Pink construction paper
- Crayons or markers
- Hole punch
- Glue

- Scissors
- Pencil
- String or yarn

Directions

1. Paint the back of the paper plate brown. Draw two big eyes and a mouth on the plate, and use the scissors to cut them out.

2. Cut out two small round ears from the brown construction paper, and glue them close to the top of the plate. Cut a small circle from the pink construction paper to make a nose, and glue it in place.

3. Cut small bits of string or yarn to make the whiskers, and glue them in place. Punch a hole on each side of the mask. Cut string or yarn, run them through the holes, and tie them into place. Now you can tie on your mask!

31. Solar System Model

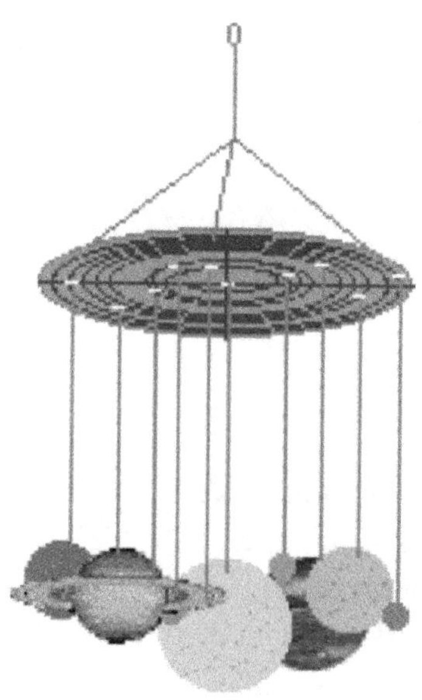

Materials

- Round piece of cardboard about 1 foot across (the cardboard from a frozen pizza works well)
- Scissors
- Tape
- String
- Multiple colors of construction paper
- Crayons or markers
- Compass for making circles

Directions

1. The large cardboard circle will be the top of your model. All of the planets and the sun will hang from it. Find the center of the large cardboard circle and mark it with a pencil. This will be the location of the sun.

2. Use the compass to draw the orbits of the 9 planets around the sun. The first four planets should be quite close to the sun. Then there should be a gap before placing the last 5 planets relatively close together.

3. Using the tips of the scissors, punch holes in the cardboard where the planets will hang. There should be one hole in the center for the sun, and a hole on each orbit. Space the holes out so they are not right next to one another.

4. Cut circles from the construction paper to make the planets. Jupiter, Saturn, Uranus, and Neptune should be the largest. The rest should be much smaller.

5. Cut a hole in the top of each planet and secure it with a piece of string. Tie the strings to the large cardboard "orbit." The sun goes in the middle. The order of planets moving outwards from the sun is Mercury, Venus, Earth, Mars, Jupiter, Saturn, Uranus, Neptune, and Pluto.

6. To hang the model, tie three pieces of string from three sides of the model. Tie those strings together, and then tie them to another string, from which you will hang the model.

32. Shoebox Guitar

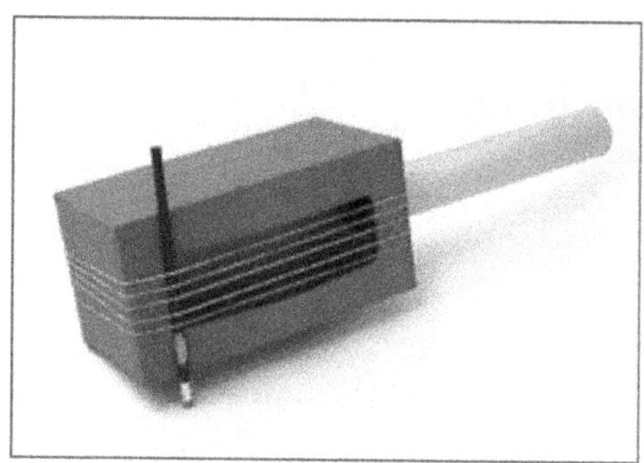

Materials

- Old shoebox with a lid
- 4 rubber bands
- Pencil
- Paper towel tube
- Glue or tape

Directions

1. Lay the shoebox lid on the ground or table horizontally. Cut an oval into the shoebox lid (or ask an adult to do this part). Tape the lid onto the shoebox. Wrap the rubber bands from one end of the shoebox to the other so they cross the oval lengthwise.

2. Place the pencil under the rubber bands on one end of the shoebox. On the other end of the shoebox, tape or glue the paper towel holder to make the handle. Play your guitar!

33. Rainstick

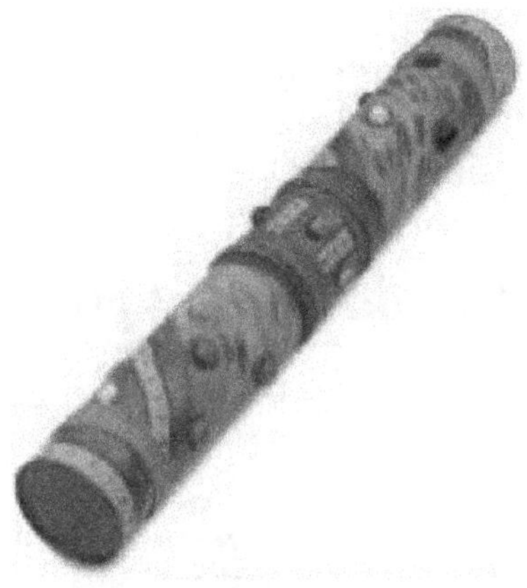

Materials

- Paper towel tube
- Aluminum foil
- Small dried beans
- Brown paper
- Glue
- Scissors
- Crayons or markers

Directions

1. Trace around the end of your tube onto a piece of brown paper. Then, draw a bigger circle around the first. Cut out the bigger circle. Draw lines connecting the two circles, then cut along these lines to make spokes. Use the spokes to attach the "lid" to one end of the paper towel tube.

2. Cut two strips of aluminum foil that are about 1 ½ times the length of the paper towel tube and 6" across. Roll these aluminum foil strips into two long pieces, and then twist them into a spring shape. Put the aluminum foil "springs"

into the paper towel tube. Fill the tube about 1/10 with dried beans.

3. Secure the other end of the tube using the same method. Use crayons or markers to decorate your rainstick, and then shake, shake, shake!

34. Plastic and Yarn Picture Frame

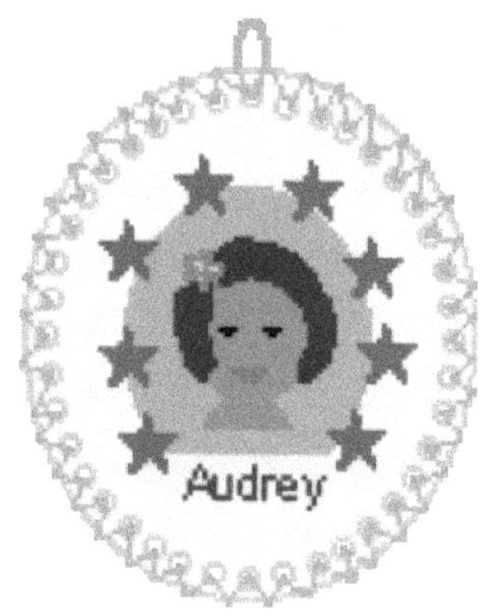

Materials

- Thick, flexible, clear plastic
- Photo to frame
- Hole punch
- Yarn
- Scissors
- Glue
- Stickers
- Thick needle (optional) or clear nail polish

Directions

1. Write the date on the back of the photo along with the names of everyone in it. You will be able to read this once the photo is framed.

2. Lay the photo on the plastic. Measure about an inch around the picture, and cut out the plastic at that marker. Then cut a second piece of plastic the same size as the first. One piece will be for the front of the frame. The second will be for the back.

3. Put the two pieces of plastic together (without the picture) and use the hole punch to make holes all around the outside of the frame.

4. Place the photo on one piece of plastic and use a bit of glue to dab it in place. Put stickers around this piece as desired. Place the second piece of plastic over the first so the holes match up perfectly.

5. Cut a long piece of yard to loop it in and out of the holes to "sew" the frame together. Older children can use the needle. Otherwise, dab a little clear polish to the end to secure it and use it as a needle.

6. Cut a final hole in the top of the frame, and attach a piece of yarn to hang the picture.

35. Colorful Cloud Dough

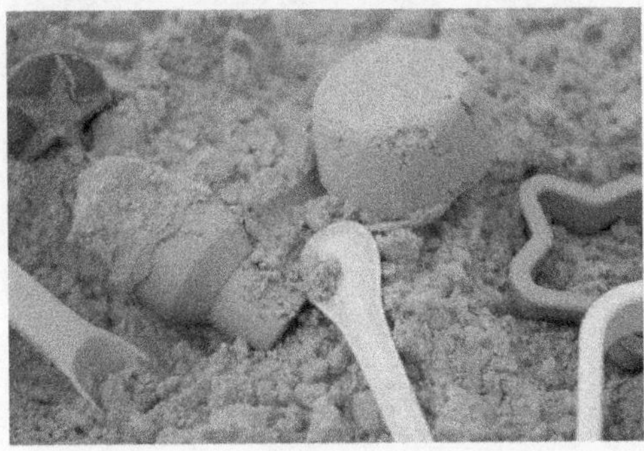

Materials

- Flour

- Oil
- Oil or gel based food coloring
- Glitter or essential oils (optional)

Directions

1. First decide how much cloud dough you would like. For every cup of oil, you will need eight cups of flour. Scale it down to fit your needs.

2. Combine the oil and food coloring. They won't exactly blend, but they will combine in a way that makes it easiest to blend with the flour.

3. Add the flour and fully mix it together with your hands. If you'd like essential oils or glitter, incorporate them with the completed mixture. Play with the dough! Form it into "cookies," or roll it out with a rolling pin. Have fun!

36. Fireworks in A Jar

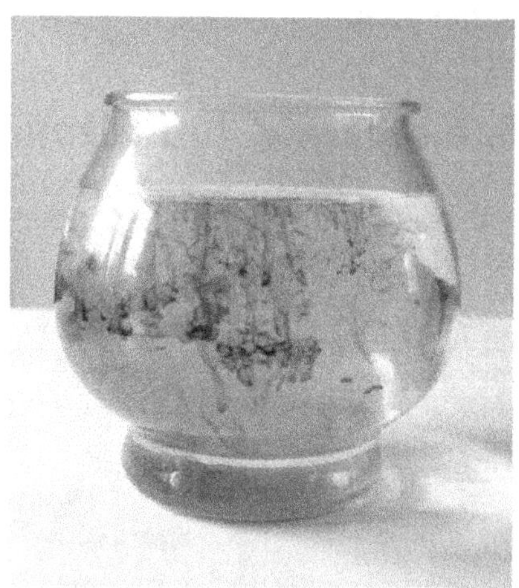

Materials

- Cooking oil

- Liquid food coloring
- Small container
- Glass of warm water
- Fork

Directions

1. Add a few tablespoons of oil to the small container. Drop in different colors of liquid food coloring. Use the fork to agitate the food coloring and break it up into smaller beads within the container.

2. Slowly pour the mixture into the jar of warm water so the oil rests on top of the water. Watch as the oil slowly drops into the water. Enjoy the fireworks show!

37. Family Tree

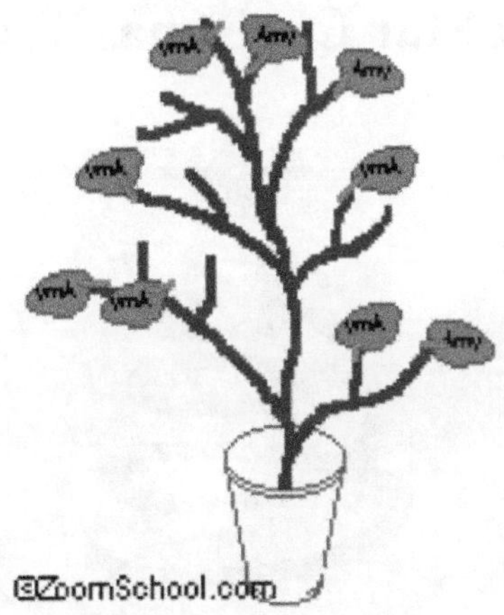

Materials

- Sky blue and green construction paper
- Markers
- Twig with many branches (from your yard)
- Scissors
- Yarn

- Hole punch
- Styrofoam or paper cup
- Glue stick
- Lump of play dough or other clay

Directions

1. Put the lump of clay inside the cup, and stick the long end of the twig into the clay so the branches come out like a small tree. Cut out big leaves from the green construction paper. Cut enough for all of the people in the child's family.

2. Write the name of each person on the leaf with the marker. Punch a hole on the tip of each leaf. Use the yarn to attach each leaf to the tree. Put the oldest generation toward the base (or the roots) of the tree. Each generation after should be higher on the tree, with the child at the top.

38. Shooting Star Christmas Tree Ornament

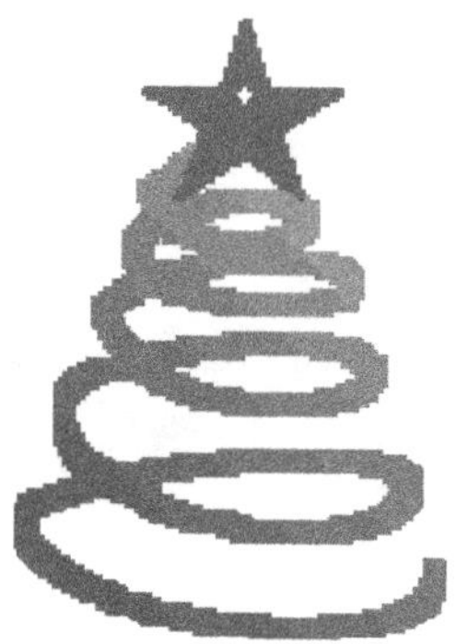

Materials

- Small thick piece of paper, felt, or other easy to cut material (up to two colors)
- Glue
- Hole punch
- Mug

- Hole punch reinforcements
- Scissors
- Pencil
- Glitter
- Yarn
- Markers

Directions

1. Cut a circle from the paper or felt. Use the coffee mug as a template. Starting at the edge of the circle cut a spiral going to the middle of the circle. Decorate the paper with glitter or markers. Cut a small star (about 1"-2" wide) and punch a hole at the top. Decorate it with glitter or markers.

2. Use reinforcement to bolster the hole, since this is what the ornament will hang from. Glue the star to the center of the spiral circle, and let the coils release. Run a bit of yarn through the hole in the star, and hang the ornament on your tree!

39. Pinecone Bird Feeder

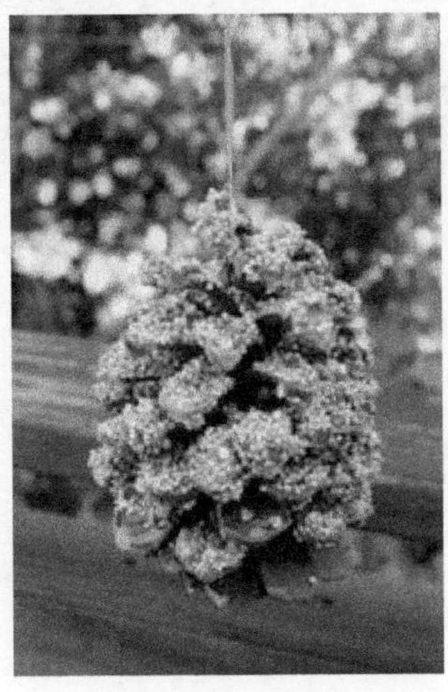

Materials

- Large open pinecone
- Vegetable shortening or lard
- Oats or corn meal
- Birdseed
- A few feet of string

Directions

1. Mix ½ cup of the shortening or lard with 2 ½ cups of the cornmeal or oats. Roll the pinecone in the mixture, and then roll it in the birdseed.

2. Tie the string to the tip of the pinecone, and suspend it from a tree in your yard.

40. Paper Chain Caterpillar

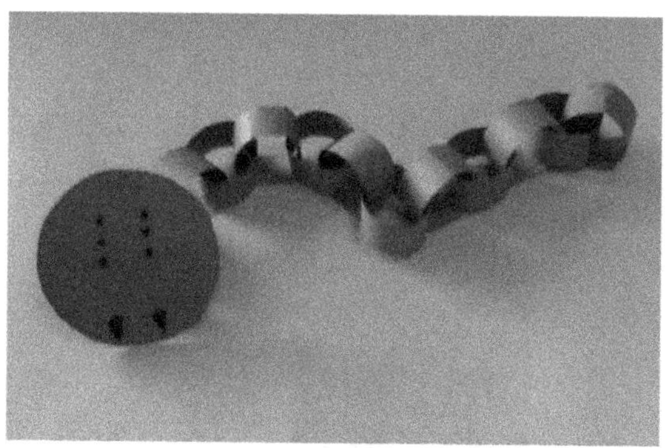

Materials

- Construction paper
- Scissors
- Glue stick
- Markers or crayons
- Optional string

Directions

1. Cut the construction paper into thirteen strips that are 1" x 6", and one piece that is 4" square. Form one of the strips into a circle, and secure it with glue.

2. Form another strip into a circle looping through the first circle, and secure it with glue again. Repeat this process for all thirteen strips. Cut a circle from the paper square to make the head of the caterpillar. Using the marker or crayon, draw on some caterpillar eyes.

3. With the scrap paper leftover, cut out two tiny triangles, and glue them to the bottom of the head. These are the mandibles. Caterpillars use them to eat leaves. Glue the head to the caterpillar.

41. Egg Carton Camel

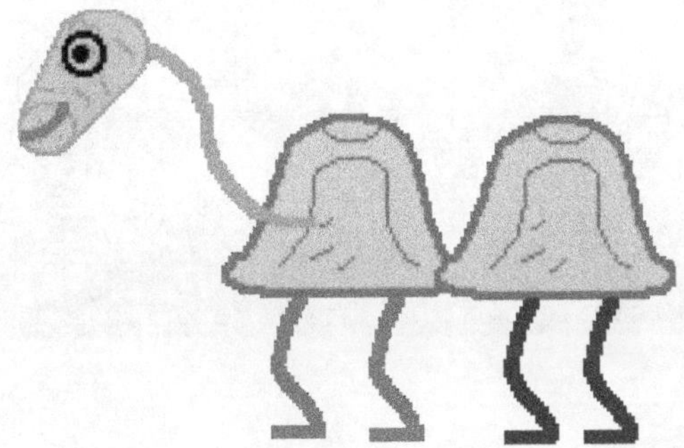

Materials

- Egg carton
- Scissors
- Pipe cleaners
- Cork
- Black marker

Directions

1. Cut out two of the pockets of the egg carton so they are still connected. Discard the rest of the carton. Use the scissors to puncture 4 holes in the center of the egg carton, in the top of one end for the head, and in the back for a tail (or have an adult do this step).

2. Push a pipe cleaner through each hole in the bottom for the legs and insert one in the back for the tail. Puncture a hole in the end of the cork. Push a pipe cleaner into the cork, and push the other end into the hole for the head. Draw a face on the cork.

42. Melted Crayon Butterfly Hanging

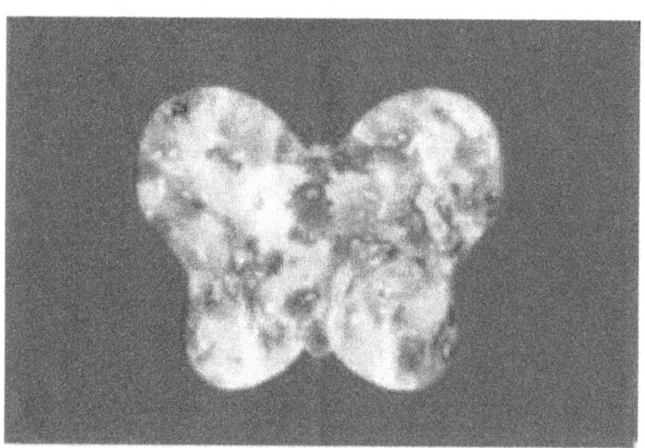

Materials

- Waxed paper
- Crayon shavings (shaved by an adult using a knife or scissors)
- Scissors
- Pencil
- Iron
- Hole punch
- Piece of string

1. Fold a piece of waxed paper in half. Draw a half of a butterfly with the body on the folded side. Flip the paper over and draw the other half of the butterfly using the first half as a template.

2. Put some crayon shavings on the paper to cover the butterfly. It's okay if they go outside of the lines. You'll cut out the butterfly shape later.

3. Cover the waxed paper with another piece of paper. Cover the two pieces of paper with a paper towel, and have an adult iron them together on low heat. Cut out the shape of the butterfly. Punch a hole at the top center or the butterfly, and attach the string to make a hanger. Display your beautiful butterfly!

43. Tie Card for Dad

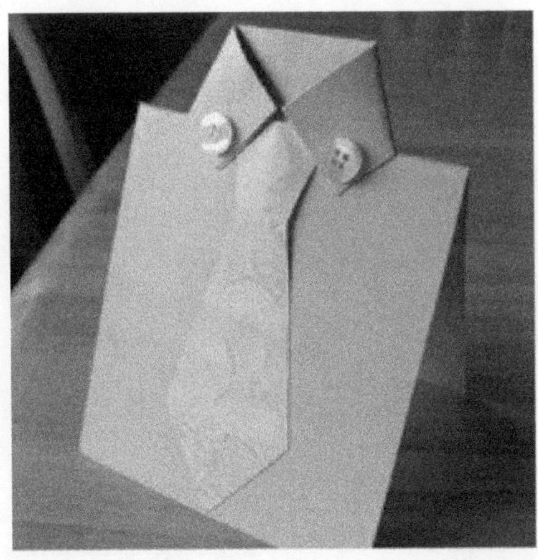

Materials

- A piece of heavy cardstock

- Scissors
- Marker
- Glue
- 5 small white shirt buttons
- A piece of colored construction paper or an old tie (ask your dad before you cut one up!)

Directions

1. Cut out the top of the cardstock into an M shape. Draw a line down the middle of the shirt. Glue the buttons in a row to the right of the line you drew. Either cut a tie from the construction paper or use the bottom of the tie you already have. Glue the top of the tie to the card so the rest can move easily.

2. Fold down the collar that you made in the M shape. Glue the remaining buttons on top of each side of the collar. Write a message to your dad on the tie, the underside of the tie, or the area of the card that the tie covers.

44. Patriotic Paperweight

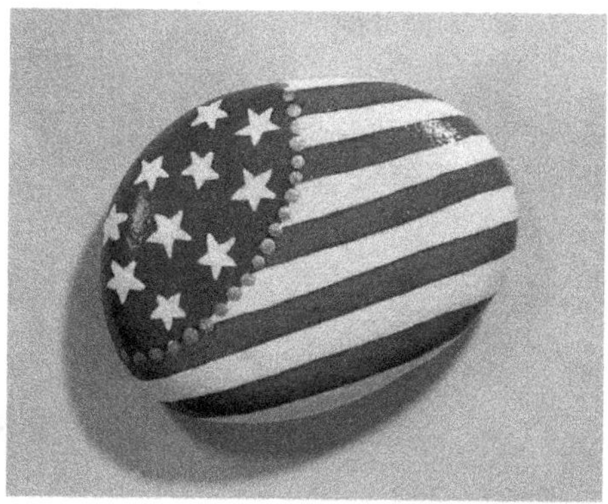

Materials

- Smooth flat stone

- Pencil
- Red, white, and blue paint
- Paintbrush
- Acrylic varnish

Directions

1. Use the pencil to mark off the left corner of the rock. This will be where the stars will be on the flag. Paint inside the corner you just drew with the blue paint. Paint the rest of the rock white. Let the rock completely dry. Paint on red stripes over the white section.

2. Paint white stars over the blue section. Coat the entire rock with the acrylic varnish to seal the paint and make it shiny. Use your rock as a paperweight or just as decoration.

45. Pasta Skeleton

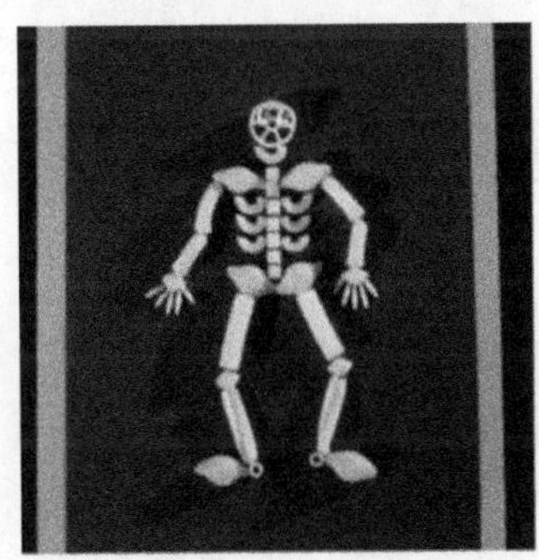

Materials

- Black construction paper
- White glue
- White marker or crayon (optional)
- Different types of dried beans and pasta (the more shapes the better!)

Directions

1. Arrange the pasta and beans onto the black paper in the shape of a skeleton. Penne pasta works well for the arms and legs. Wagon wheels work well for the head. Spaghetti or angel hair can be used for the fingers and toes.

2. Once you are happy with the arrangement, glue the pieces down. If you'd like, you can use the white marker or crayon to label the bones.

46. Hawaiian Flower Lei

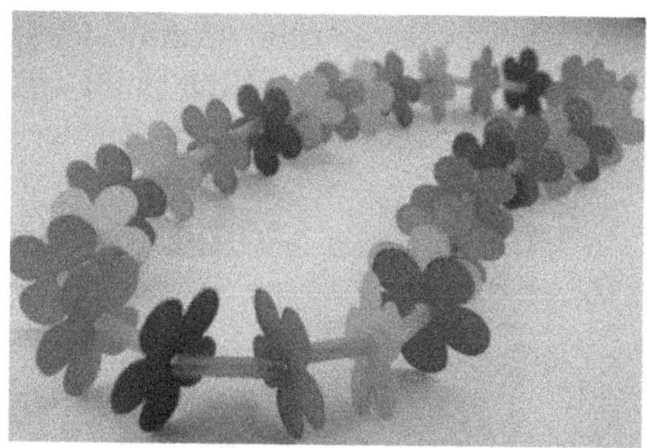

Materials

- Thick paper
- Drinking straws
- Scissors
- Yarn
- Paint, markers, or glitter (optional)

Directions

1. Cut out many flowers from the construction paper. If you want to, decorate the flowers with the markers, paint, or glitter. Piece a hole in the middle of each flower with the scissors.

2. Cut the drinking straws into 1-½ inch segments. These will go between the flowers in the necklace. Cut a piece of yarn about 2 feet long. Tie a big knot into one end of the yarn. Thread the other end through a flower, then a piece of straw.

3. Keep threading the flowers and straw onto the yarn until all of the flowers are gone. Tie the ends together, and enjoy your lei!

47. I Spy Bottle

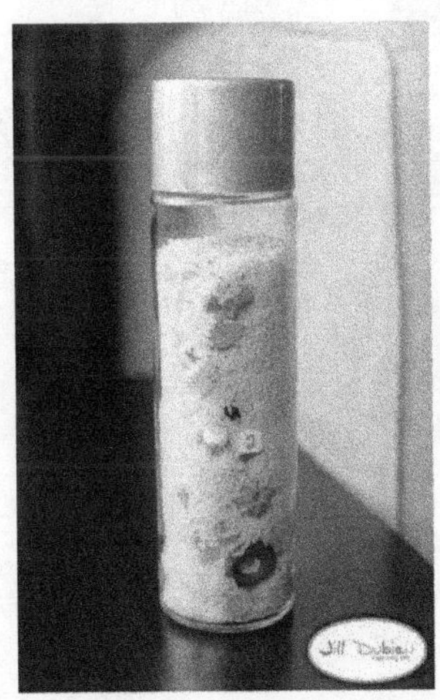

Materials

- Plastic bottle with a lid
- Small objects that will fit inside the bottle
- Rice or sand
- Funnel
- Hot glue gun and glue

Directions

1. Place all of the objects inside the bottle. Use the funnel to fill the bottle ¾ full of sand or rice.

2. Glue the lid onto the bottle. Enjoy moving the bottle around to find all of the objects inside.

48. Paper Mache Vase

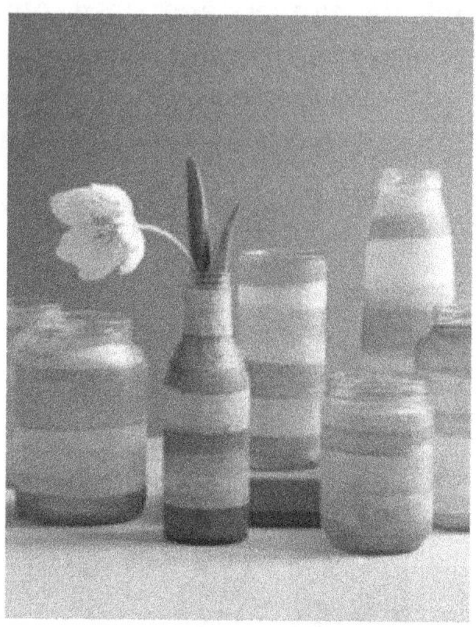

Materials

- Empty, clean water bottle
- Newspaper
- Flour and water
- Pan and stirrer
- Colored tissue paper
- Clear varnish

Directions

1. Mix ½ cup of flour with ½ cup water to make a thin paste. Stir the mixture into 2 cups of boiling water. Simmer for three minutes, and then let the water cool. Cut up the newspaper into many 1" strips. Remove the top cap from the bottle.

2. Dip the strips of newspaper into the "glue" and stick them to the bottle. Completely cover the sides of the bottle, but leave the top and bottom clean. Let the bottle dry completely (overnight).

3. Decorate the dry vase with paper mache tissue paper. Allow the tissue paper to dry, and seal the vase with the varnish.

49. Flowerpot Pen Holder

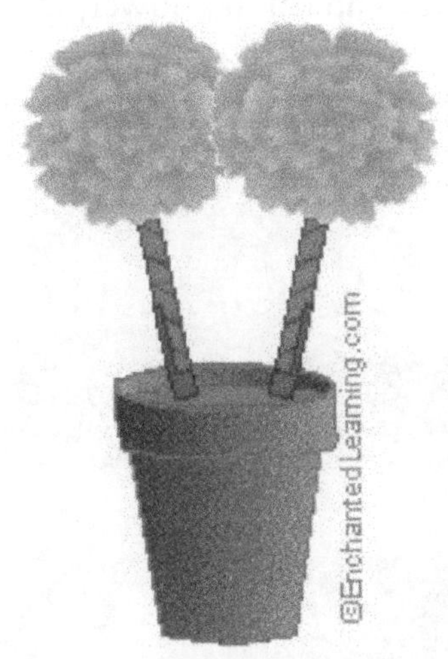

Materials

- Small unglazed clay flowerpot
- Plaster of Paris
- Large bowl and stirrer
- Ballpoint pen with a top
- Green paint
- Paintbrush
- Green florist tape
- Tissue paper
- Disposable rubber gloves
- Hot glue gun and glue

Directions

1. Have an adult mix enough Plaster of Paris to almost fill the flowerpot. Once the plaster is firm but not yet hard, push the pen cap into the plaster with the opening facing out. Once it dries, paint the plaster green. Wrap the pen with the green florist tape.

2. Bunch up the tissue paper to make a flower, and glue it to the end of the pen with the hot glue gun. Now you can put the pen back into the cap (in the flowerpot).

50. Valentine's Day Heart Wreath

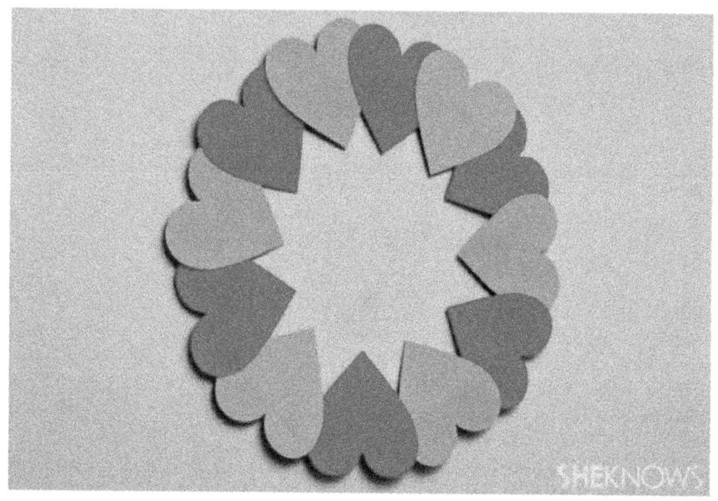

Materials

- Red and pink construction paper
- Paper plate
- Scissors
- Glue
- Glitter (optional)

Directions

1. Cut a large hole in the paper plate so only the outside inch remains. Cut the red and pink construction paper into hearts.

2. Glue the hearts to the edges of the paper plate so they overlap. If you'd like, add a thin layer of glue and shake the glitter over the hearts.

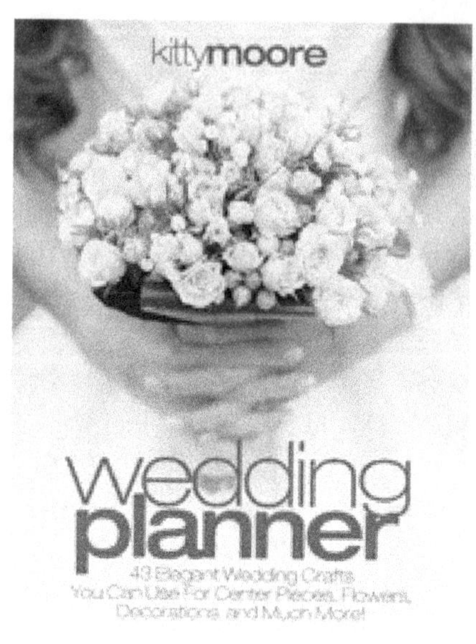

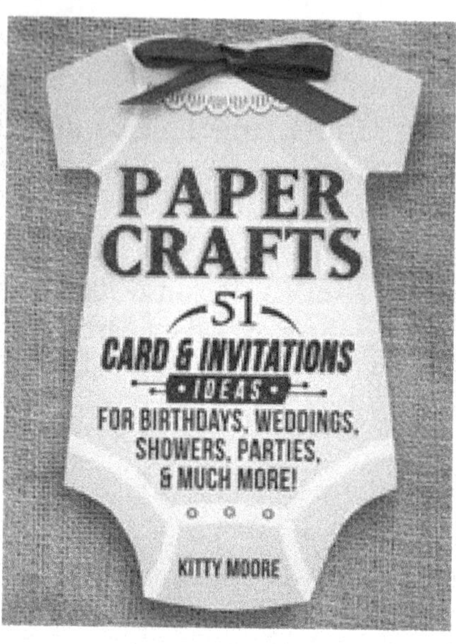

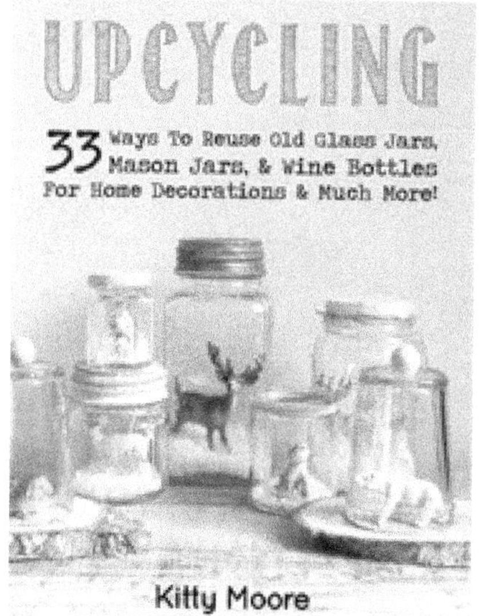

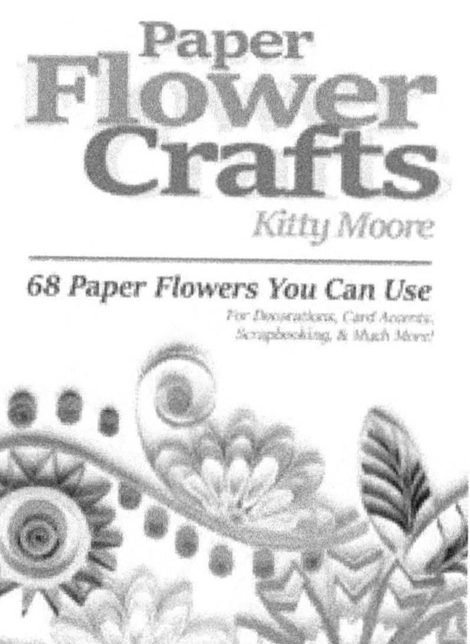

Check out Kitty's books at:

ArtsCraftsAndMore.com/go/books

51. Japanese Kokeshi Doll

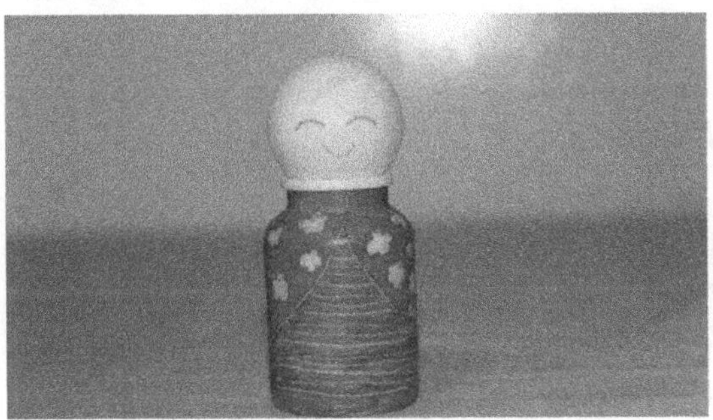

Materials

- Ping-pong ball
- Small clean label-less bottle (vitamin bottles work well)
- Hot glue gun and glue
- Acrylic paint
- Paintbrush
- Marker

Directions

1. Hot glue the ping-pong ball to the top of the bottle. Let the glue dry completely (a few minutes). Brush the paint onto the bottle. This is the doll's dress. Draw on a face and hair to the ping-pong ball. Use markers to decorate the body to make a beautiful kimono.

52. Fire Truck Snacks

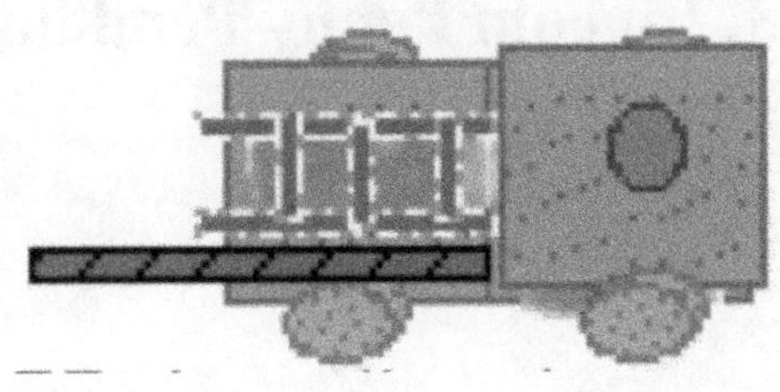

Materials

- Paper plate
- Graham crackers (1 ½ per truck)
- Tiny Ritz crackers
- Stick pretzels
- Black licorice
- Soft cream cheese or frosting
- Red food coloring
- A red jellybean, strawberry, or dot

Directions

1. Mix a few drops of food coloring into the cream cheese or frosting. You will use this to "glue" your fire truck together.

2. Spread the glue over one side of the whole graham cracker. Then stick the half graham cracker on one half of the whole one. This is the cab of the fire truck.

3. "Glue" the red jellybean, dot, or strawberry onto the middle of the cab. This is the truck's red light. "Glue" four small Ritz "wheels" to the sides of the graham cracker.

4. On the other side of the whole graham cracker (not the cab side), "glue" two pretzels to make the ladder. Glue in broken pretzel pieces to make the ladder steps.

5. "Glue" a piece of licorice under the ladder. This is the fire hose. Now, play with your food! Then eat it.

53. Lincoln Penny Pendant

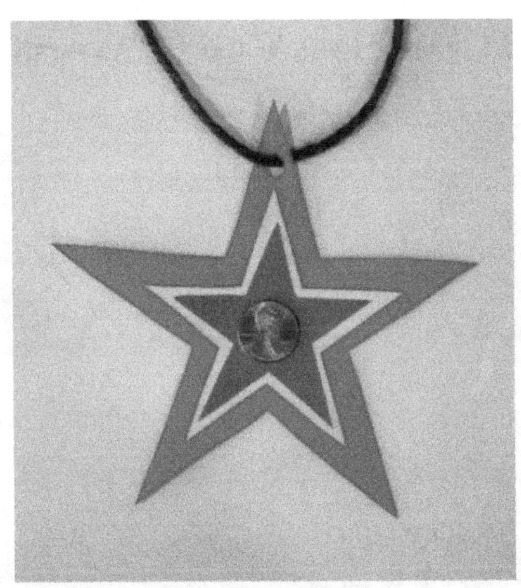

Materials

- Penny
- Construction paper (red, white, and blue)
- White glue or glue stick
- Scissors
- Hole punch
- Yarn

Directions

1. Cut out three stars (one red, one white, and one blue). The red should be the biggest. The white should be slightly smaller, and the blue should be the smallest.

2. Glue the white star onto the red star. Then, glue the blue star on top of the white star. Glue the penny in the middle of the blue star. Punch a hole in the top of the star. String the yarn through the hole to make a necklace. Wear your pendant on the 4th of July or President's Day!

54. Delicious Cup O' Worms

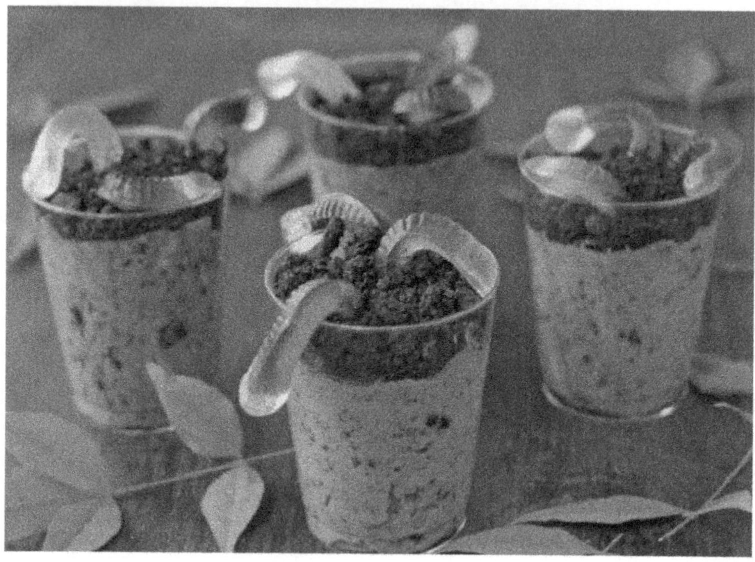

Materials

- Chocolate pudding
- Gummy worms
- Cocoa powder
- Chocolate sprinkles
- Clear plastic cup

Directions

1. Fill the cup about 3/4 with pudding. Sprinkle some cocoa powder and chocolate sprinkles over the pudding to almost fill the cup.

2. Push the ends of a few worms into the "soil" so it looks like they are crawling out of the ground. Refrigerate until you're ready to devour your worms!

55. Paper Bag Christmas Stocking

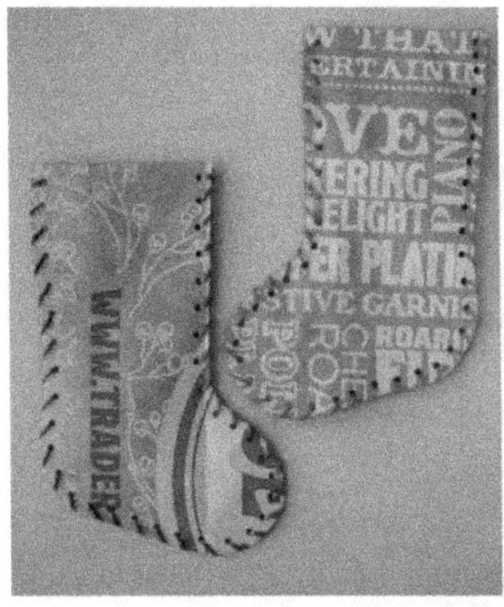

Materials

- Thick brown paper (like from a paper bag)
- Pencil
- Scissors
- Glue
- Hole punch
- Yarn
- Markers or crayons

Directions

1. Draw a stocking on the brown paper. Cut out two copies of the stocking. Glue the two stockings together along the edges. Do not put any glue along the top opening or the inside of the stocking. Punch holes around the sides and bottom of the stocking.

2. Weave the yarn through the holes to "sew" the stocking together. Leave a loop at the top left of the stocking to hang it. Decorate your stocking with markers or crayons.

56. Real Crystal Snowflake

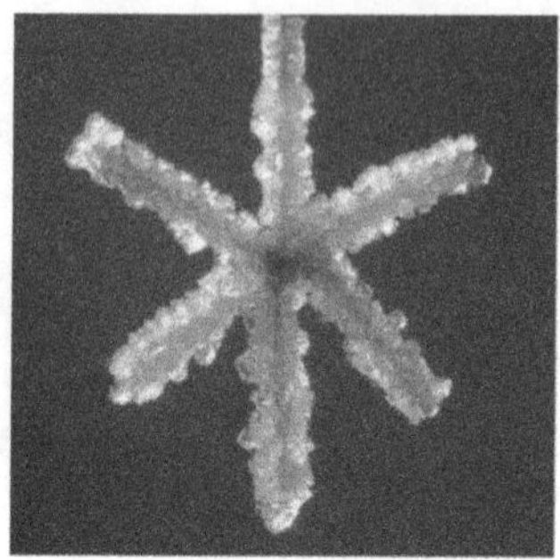

Materials

- Wide mouthed jar
- 3 white pipe cleaners
- String
- Scissors
- Pencil
- Boiling water (make sure an adult does this part)
- Spoon
- Borax
- Blue food coloring (optional)

Directions

1. Arrange the three pipe cleaners to make a six-point snowflake. Twist them together at the middle. Make sure the snowflake fits inside the jar.

2. Tie the string around the pipe cleaners to make a snowflake shape. Snowflakes are unique, so the pattern can be whatever you like. Trim off the excess string.

3. Tie a small bit of string to the end of one of the pipe cleaners, and tie the other end of string to a pencil. Hang the snowflake inside the jar so it doesn't hit the bottom. The pencil will sit

on top of the jar. Once you get the length right, remove the pencil and snowflake from the jar.

4. Have an adult fill the empty jar with boiling water. Add the borax to the jar and stir with a spoon. Add enough to get a super saturated mixture (about 3 tablespoons per cup of water).

5. If desired, drop in a few drops of blue food coloring, Place the snowflake inside the jar, and wait at least overnight. In the morning, you will have a beautiful snowflake!

57. Paper Bag Cat Puppet

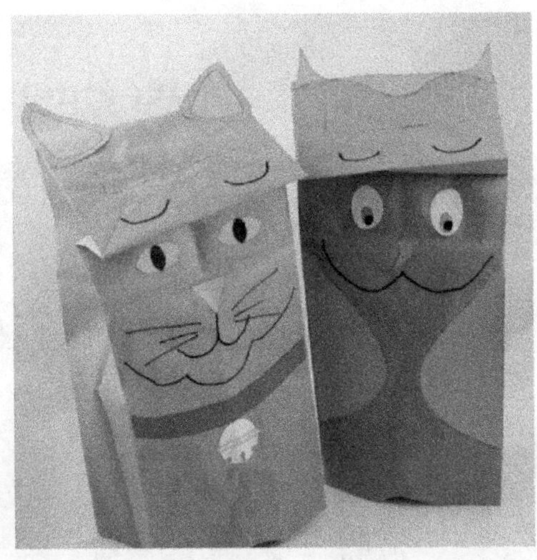

Materials

- Paper lunch bag
- Scraps of construction paper
- Glue
- Scissors
- Markers or crayons
- Googly eyes and pipe cleaners (optional)

Directions

1. Fold the bag up so it can lay flat with the bottom fold facing up. Fold under the two edges of the bottom of the bag to make the cat's snout.

2. Cut out ears, paws, and a nose from the construction paper. Glue them onto the cat. If you'd like, you can use pipe cleaners for whiskers. If not, cut out some paper for the whiskers and glue them in place.

3. Attach the googly eyes if you're using them. If not, cut out some kitty eyes. Put your hand inside the paper bag. You now have a puppet!

58. Plastic Egg Easter Bunny

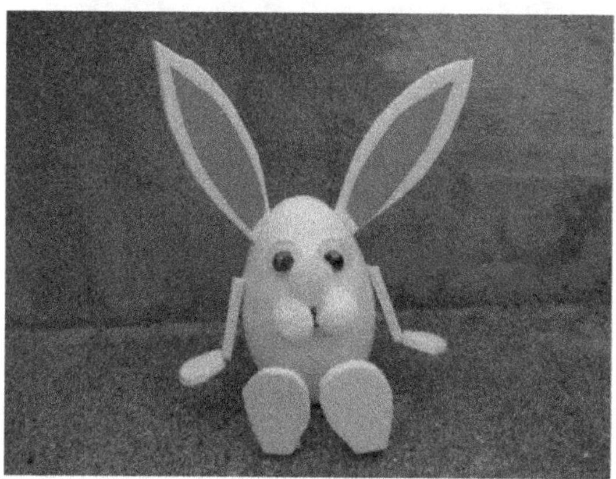

Materials

- Pipe cleaners
- Scissors
- Plastic egg
- One or two white pompoms
- One pink pompom
- Hot glue

- White and pink construction paper
- 2 googly eyes

Directions

1. Cut two large white bunny ears from the construction paper. Then, cut two smaller ears from the pink paper. Glue the pink ears into the white ears. Glue the ears to the top of the small end of the egg. Glue the two white pompoms just above the place where the egg opens up. These are the bunny's cheeks.

2. Glue the small pink pompom above the white pompoms. This is the bunny's nose. Glue the googly eyes into place. If you like, fill your bunny with small pieces of candy.

59. String of Leaves

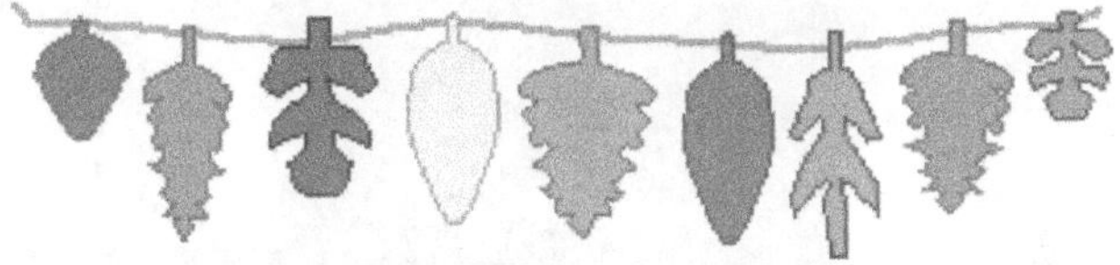

Materials

- String
- Construction paper
- Scissors
- Crayons or markers
- Glue, tape, or stapler

Directions

1. Cut out many leaves from the construction paper. Make them different shapes and colors if you'd like. Make sure your leaves have thick, long stems, since that is where they will hang from the string.

2. Fold the stems in half toward the body of the leaves. Glue, tape, or staple them in place. Run the string through the loops you just made with the stems. Hang your string somewhere in your house to welcome the fall! This is also a great decoration for Thanksgiving.

60. Dragonfly Clothespin Magnet

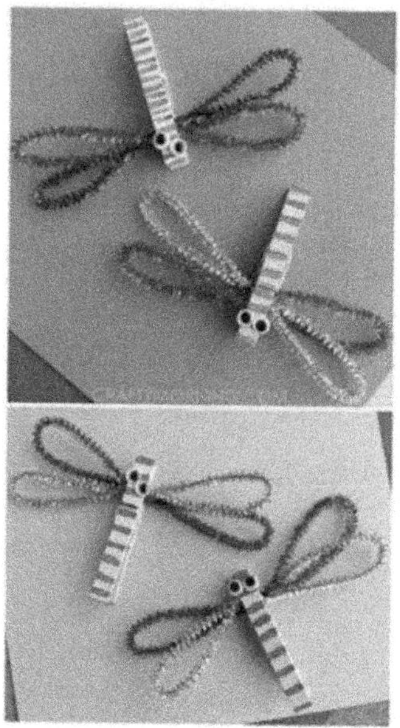

Materials

- Clothespin
- Pipe cleaners
- Markers
- Super glue
- Magnet
- Googly eyes

Directions

1. Glue two googly eyes to the end of the clothespin where it clamps down. Create two large dragonfly wings with the pipe

cleaners. Glue them to the inside of the mouth of the clothespin.

2. Decorate the clothespin how you'd like with the markers. You can draw designs on the dragonfly's body, or make it a solid color. Super glue the magnet to the back of the clothespin. Hang it on your refrigerator.

61. Melted Bead Bowl

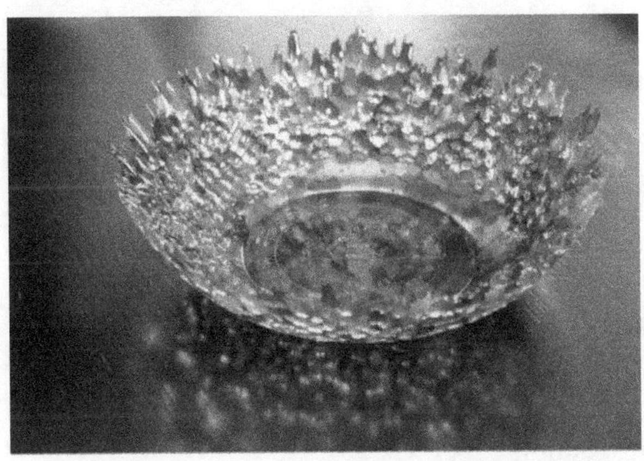

Materials

- Beads (all colors and sizes)
- Large oven safe bowl
- Pam or grease for the bowl

Directions

1. Preheat the oven to 350 degrees Fahrenheit. Spray the inside of the bowl thoroughly with Pam, or use grease and a paper towel.

2. Empty the beads into the bowl, and press them into the bottom to make a single layer that covers the bottom and runs up the sides of the bowl. Heat in the oven for 15 minutes.

Once the bowl has cooled, peel away the bead bowl from inside. Fill the bowl with whatever you want!

62. Salt and Watercolor Painting

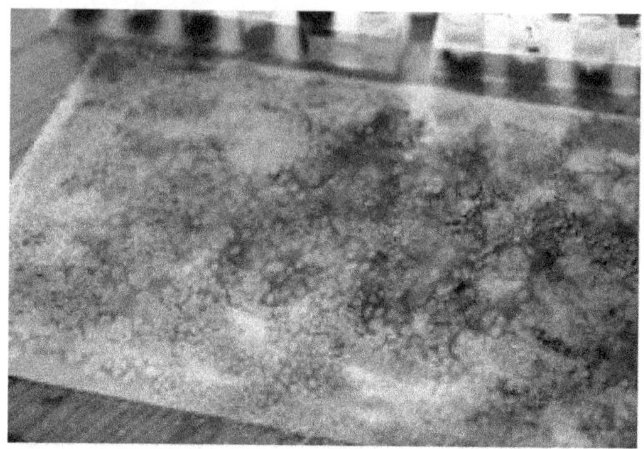

Materials

- Salt
- Construction paper
- Elmer's glue
- Watercolors
- Eyedropper

Directions

1. Apply glue to the construction paper. The glue should be in a thick line all over the paper. Make any design you wish. Cover the glue with salt. Shake off the excess salt.

2. Use the eyedropper to add liquid watercolors to the salt. Drop small droplets in the salt. It will spread out along the line of glue. Use all different watercolors to make fun and unique patterns. Allow the painting to fully dry.

63. Homemade Sidewalk Chalk

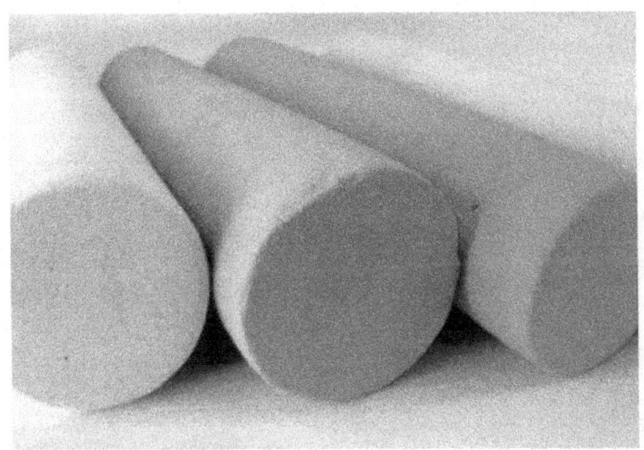

Materials

- Toilet paper tubes
- Scissors
- Plastic spoon
- Duct tape
- Small bucket (to mix the recipe)
- Waxed paper
- ¾ cup warm water
- 1 ½ cups Plaster of Paris
- 2-3 tempera paint
- Drop cloth, newspaper, or anything else to contain the mess

Directions

1. Cover one end of each toilet paper tube with duct tape to hold the contents inside. Cut as many pieces of waxed paper as you have tubes.

2. Roll each piece of waxed paper loosely, and put them inside the tubes to roughly line them. The paper should be longer than the tube.

3. Pour the warm water into the bucket. Sprinkle in the Plaster of Paris, and stir it with a plastic spoon. Mix the tempera paint in with the Plaster of Paris mixture. If you want to make multiple colors, divide the mix into several bowls, and add the colors separately.

4. Stand each tube with the tape side down on a cookie sheet or other flat surface where it can sit and dry for several days. Carefully pour the mixture into the waxed paper liners.

5. Lightly tap each tube to release any air bubbles. Allow the tubes to fully dry. It could take several days. On the last day, remove the tape so the bottom side can dry. Remove the dry chalk from the tubes, and peel away the waxed paper.

64. Sponge Octopus Bath Toy

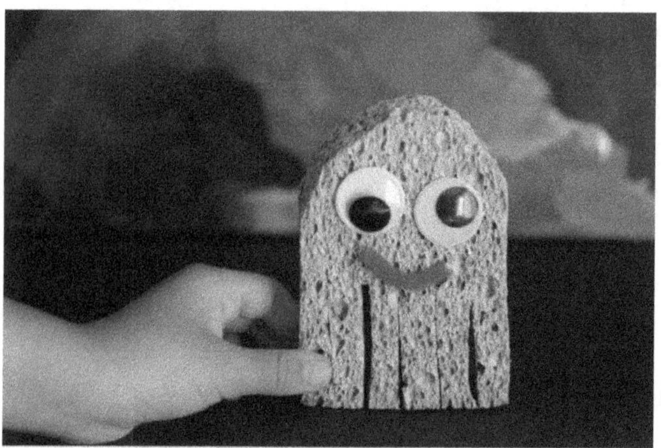

Materials

- Sponge
- Scissors
- Hot glue gun and glue
- Googly eyes
- Pipe cleaner

Directions

1. Cut the corners off the top of the sponge to make the octopus' round head. Cut strips from the bottom of the sponge to halfway up the sponge to make the octopus' many legs.

2. Glue the googly eyes in place. Cut a piece of pipe cleaner to make a smiling mouth. Glue it in place.

65. Fast and Easy Silly Putty

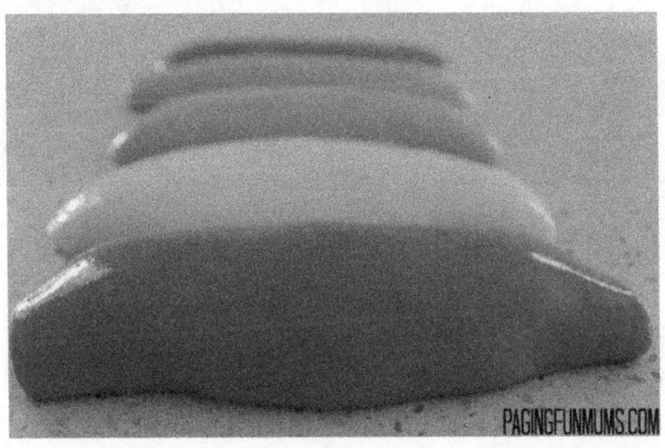

Materials

- Liquid starch
- Elmer's all-purpose glue
- A mixing bowl
- A large spoon
- Food coloring (optional)

Directions

1. Mix 1 part liquid starch with 2 parts glue. Pour the measured amounts into the mixing bowl, and blend them with the spoon. The mixture will begin to bubble.

2. Add the food coloring if desired. Mix until the liquid is fully incorporated. Once it's solid, knead it with your hands.

66. Origami Whale

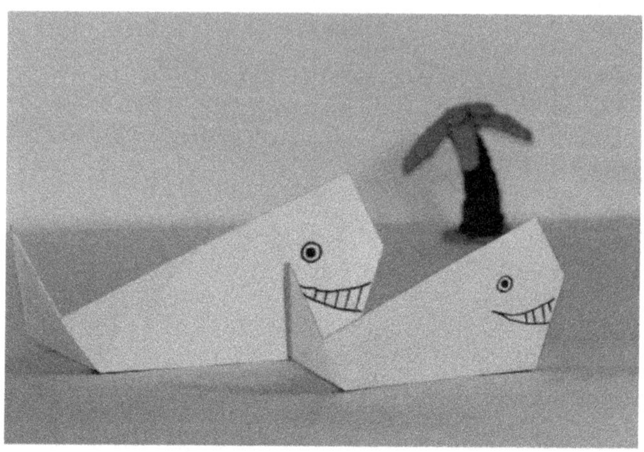

Materials

- Construction paper
- Scissors
- Markers or crayons
- Pipe cleaner

Directions

1. Start by cutting the paper in a perfect square. Fold the square in half to make a crease. Fold two opposite sides over so they meet at the crease.

2. Fold the top over to meet the other folds. Fold the tip over to meet the other folds. Fold the piece in half along the middle axis. Fold the tail up toward the ceiling.

3. Cut a slit in the tail and fold one half forward and the other half backward. Draw eyes, fins, and anything else you'd like.

67. Paper Plate Duck

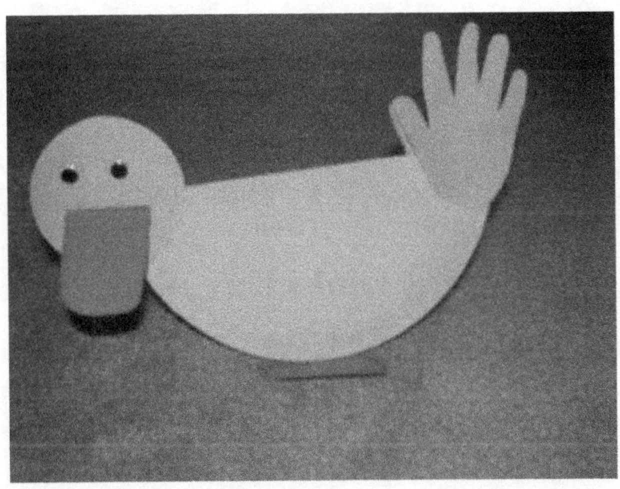

Materials

- Yellow and orange construction paper
- Paper plate
- Scissors
- Glue
- Stapler
- A pencil
- Crayon, paint, or markers
- Googly eyes

Directions

1. Trace your hands onto the yellow paper, and cut out the handprints. Fold the paper plate in half, and paint or color it yellow. Staple the hands near the fold on one end. These are the tail feathers.

2. Cut out a circle (about 3" across) from the yellow construction paper to make the duck's head. Cut the orange construction paper to make the beak. Fold back a small section at the back of the beak to glue it to the head. Staple

the duck's head to its body on the edge opposite the tail feathers. Glue on the googly eyes.

3. Using the orange construction paper cut out the duck's feet. They should have about 2" of construction paper between them so they are attached; fold the feet down to the sides. Staple the feet to the underside of the paper plate where the two edges open. Now you have a duck that can stand up!

68. April Fool's Day Banana

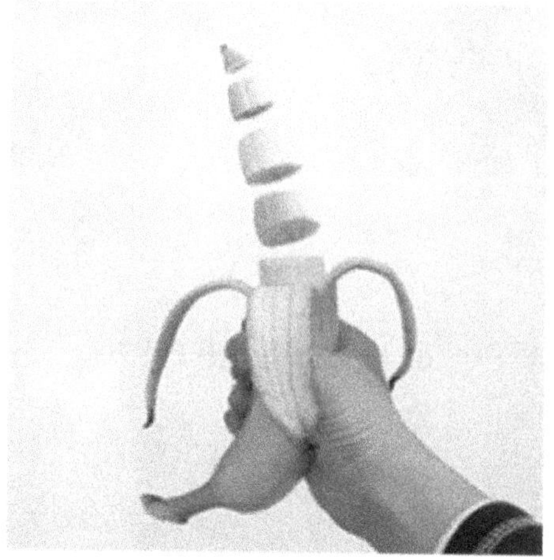

Materials

- Banana
- Toothpick

Directions

1. Push the toothpick through the top part of the banana on the seam. Start at one side and push through the flesh to slice the banana. Do not go through the peel.

2. Remove the toothpick, move down an inch, and repeat. Continue until the entire banana is sliced with the peel still

intact. Invite a friend over and have them peel the banana. They'll be amazed that it's already peeled!

69. Magazine Holder

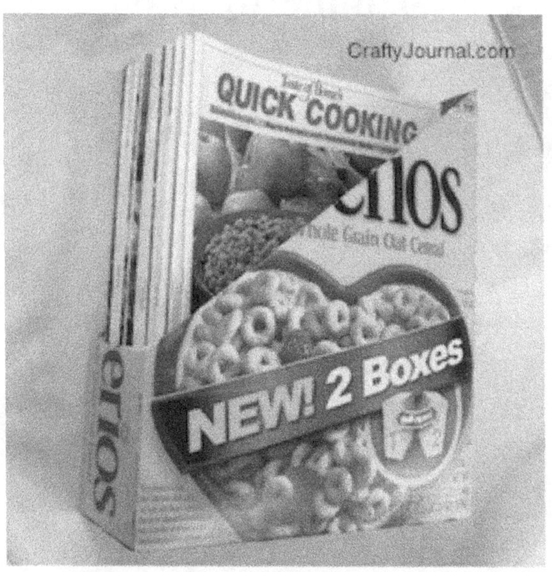

Materials

- Cereal box
- Pencil
- Ruler
- Scissors
- Old magazines
- Glue
- Small paintbrush

Directions

1. Use a pencil to mark straight lines from the top corner of the box down a slant. Cut along the line from the top of the cereal box, creating a file.

2. Cut out pictures from the magazines and use the brush to spread the glue on the back of the paper. Paste it to the box. Use the box to hold your favorite magazines.

70. Butterfly Wand

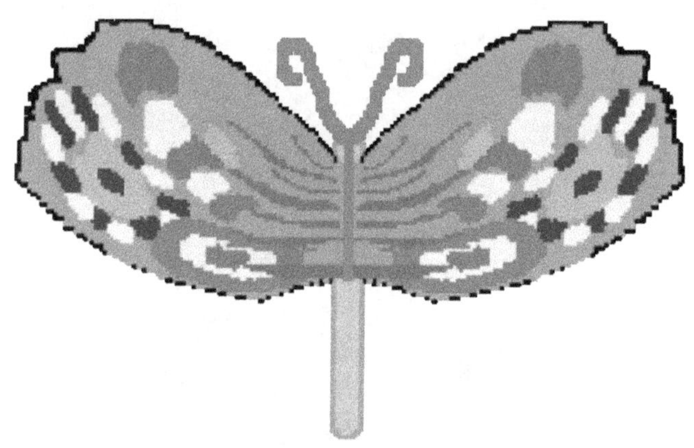

Materials

- Popsicle sticks
- 2 pipe cleaners
- Cone shaped coffee filter
- Markers or crayons
- Hot glue gun and glue

Directions

1. Glue the pipe cleaners to the popsicle stick. Open up the coffee filter at the seam. Decorate the filter with the markers or crayons. The center of the filter will be crinkled up, so concentrate on the edges.

2. Attach the wings to the popsicle stick with hot glue. Fold down the pipe cleaner to make antennae.

71. Fireworks Display

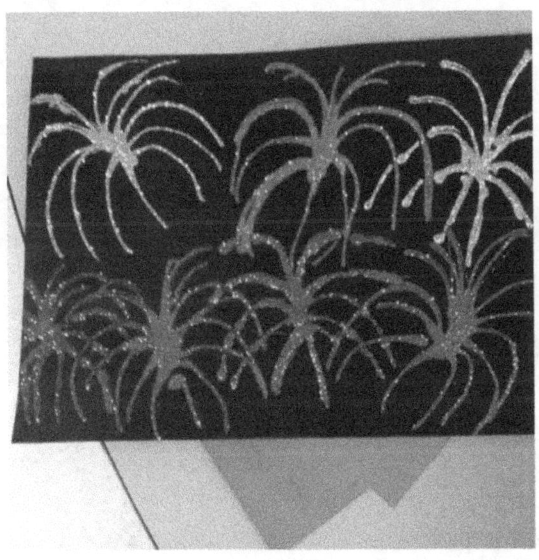

Materials

- Black or very dark construction paper
- Glitter (in several colors)
- White glue
- A straw (optional)

Directions

1. Put the glue on the construction paper in intricate shapes. If you like, you can put a large dollop of glue and use the straw to blow it in random directions.

2. Sprinkle the glitter all over the glue. Use different colors all over the paper. Shake off the excess glitter.

72. Dove of Peace

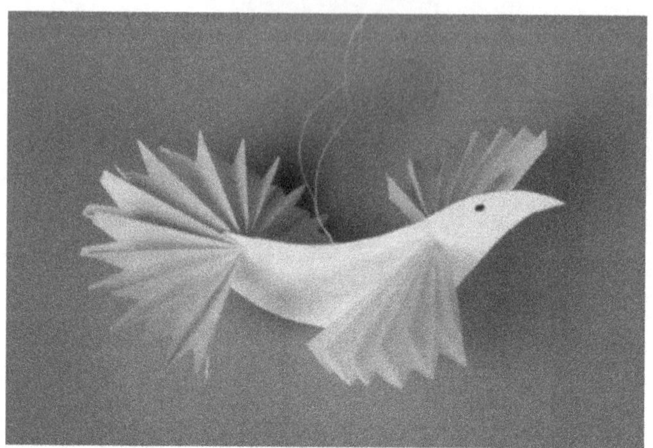

Materials

- Stiff paper
- Regular paper
- Scissors
- Pencil
- String
- Clear tape
- Markers

Directions

1. Draw the shape of a bird's body on the thick piece of paper. Cut out the paper.

2. Cut two slits in the body vertically. One should be just below the head. One should be just above the tail.

3. Cut the regular paper in half. Fold each half of the paper like an accordion.

4. Run the accordion "wings" through the slits so they are in the middle of the dove. Unfold the wings on either side of the dove.

82

5. Tape the ends of the tail together to make a fan shape. Draw eyes on the dove.

73. Pinecone Thanksgiving Turkey

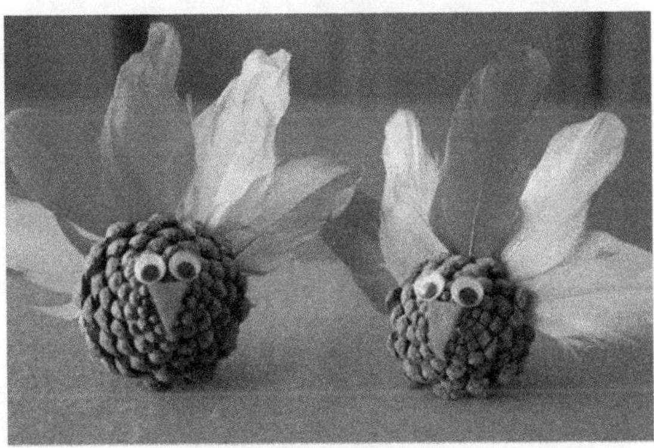

Materials

- Pinecone
- Acorn
- Brown, red, orange, and yellow construction paper
- Pencil or marker
- Scissors
- Glue
- Hot glue
- Googly eyes
- Clay

Directions

1. Cut out construction paper feathers. Put a small blob of clay on the bottom of the pinecone to keep it steady. Glue the feathers to the top wide side of the pinecone.

2. Glue the acorn to the front of the turkey with the hot glue. Glue on the googly eyes and a small piece of red construction paper for the turkey's wattle. Now you have a beautiful

decoration for Thanksgiving Day! Make sure to put the turkey on a plate so the clay doesn't stain the tablecloth.

74. Painted Mother's Day Flowerpot

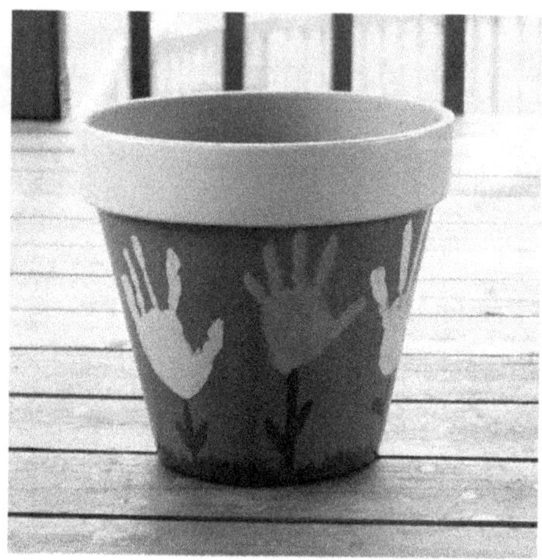

Materials

- Unglazed clay flowerpot
- Acrylic paint
- Paintbrushes
- A pack of seeds or potting soil
- Cellophane and ribbon to wrap the flowerpot (optional)

Directions

1. Use the paintbrush and paint to decorate the pot. Draw flowers, butterflies, or whatever mom loves! Allow the paint to fully dry.

2. Fill the pot with potting soil and plant the seeds. Give the plant a little water. If you'd like, wrap the pot in the cellophane, and tie it with the ribbon.

75. Frog Puppet

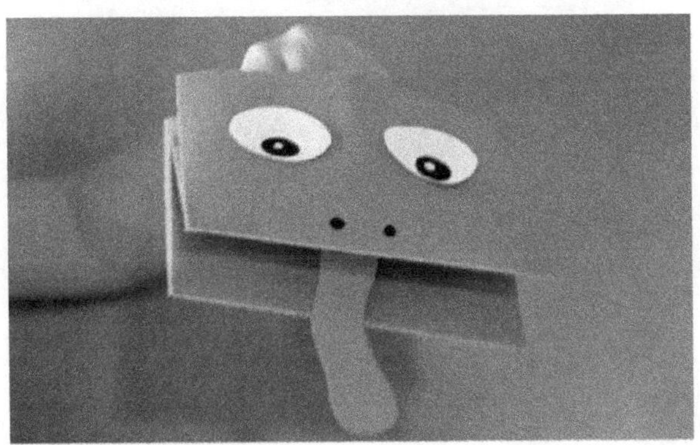

Materials

- Piece of green paper
- Piece of red paper
- Scissors
- Googly eyes
- Glue

Directions

1. Cut the green paper into a long rectangle. Fold the rectangle into a W shape. Do this by folding it in thirds lengthwise. The W is the frog. Glue googly eyes onto the top of the frog. Cut out a red tongue from the red paper.

2. Open the W from the bottom, and glue in the tongue so it sticks out. Now you can hold the puppet at the openings of the W and open and close its mouth.

76. Paper Plate Maraca

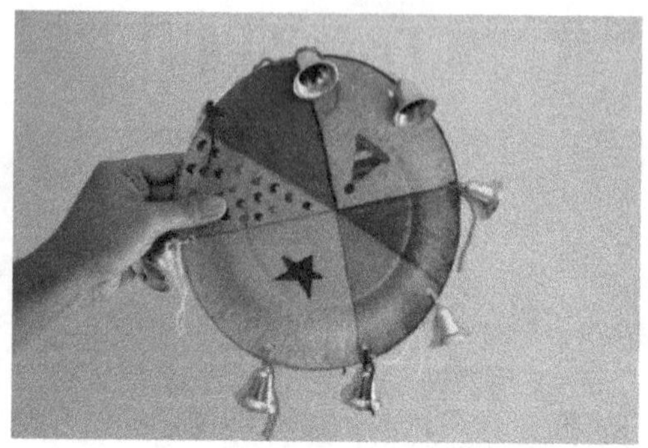

Materials

- 2 paper plates
- Dried beans, rice, or popcorn
- Stapler
- Paint and paintbrush

Directions

1. Put a handful of beans, rice, or popcorn on a paper plate. Place the other plate on top of it, and staple the two plates together.

2. Paint the maraca however you would like. Allow the paint to dry, and then shake, shake, shake!

77. Coffee Can Bank

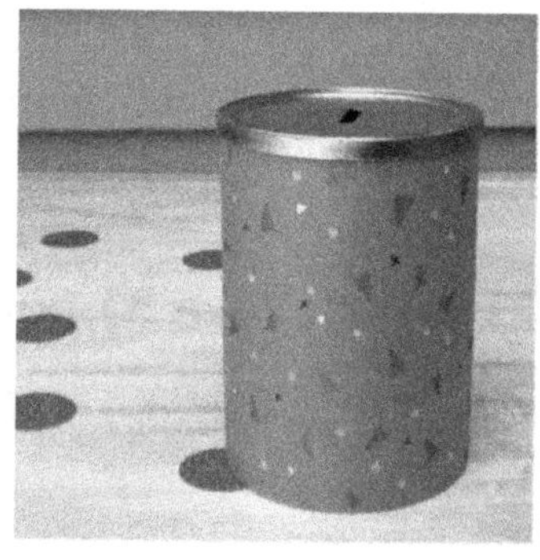

Materials

- Coffee can
- Craft knife
- Construction paper
- Scissors
- Tape measurer
- Hot glue gun and glue
- Markers, paint, stickers, glitter, or whatever you'd like to use to decorate

Directions

1. Have an adult use the craft knife to cut a slot in the lid. It should be big enough to fit any coin. Cut the construction paper in a rectangular shape that will wrap around the coffee can.

2. Lay the sheet of paper on the table, and decorate it however you like. You can use paint, markers, stickers, glitter, or anything else you can think of. Glue the paper around the can.

78. Paper Scarecrow

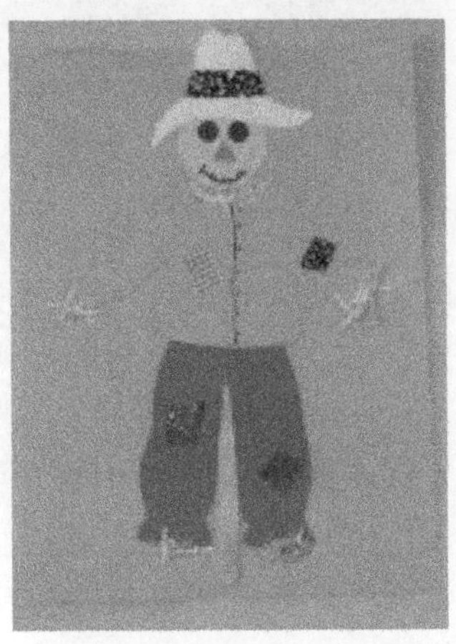

Materials

- Construction paper
- Markers or crayons
- Pencil
- Glue
- Scissors
- Googly eyes (optional)
- Real straw (optional)

Directions

1. Draw the outline of a scarecrow on the construction paper. Cut out the scarecrow's body. Draw a hat, shirt, overalls, and shoes on the construction paper. Cut them out.

2. Glue the clothes onto the scarecrow. If you'd like, glue some straw to the hands and feet. Glue on the googly eyes (if using), or draw on some eyes, a nose, and a smile.

79. Paper Towel Totem Pole

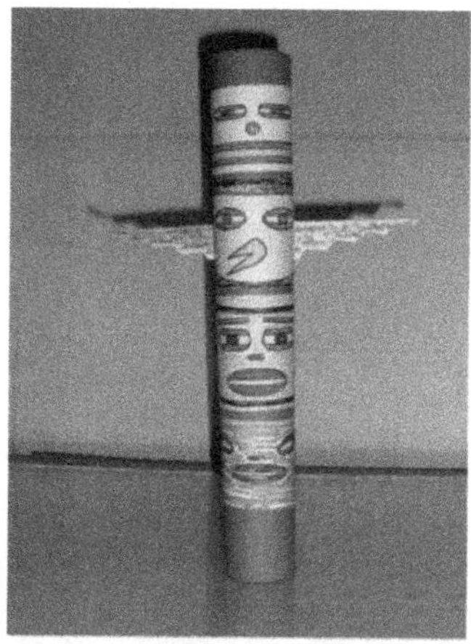

Materials

- Paper towel tube

- Crayons, tempera paint, or markers
- Brown construction paper
- Scissors
- Tape
- White glue
- 2 popsicle sticks (optional)

Directions

1. Wrap a piece of construction paper around the paper towel tube to see what size you will need. Cut the paper to size, removing any excess paper. Cut the paper into four or more horizontal strips. Draw a different animal face on each strip. Use the markers, paint, or crayons to make them colorful. Wrap the heads around the paper towel tube and glue the seams.

2. Draw wings or arms for some or all of the animals. Cut them out of the paper and glue them to the back of the totem pole so they stick out on each side. If you choose, you can glue two popsicle sticks to the bottom of the totem pole so it stands upright.

80. Leprechaun Marionette

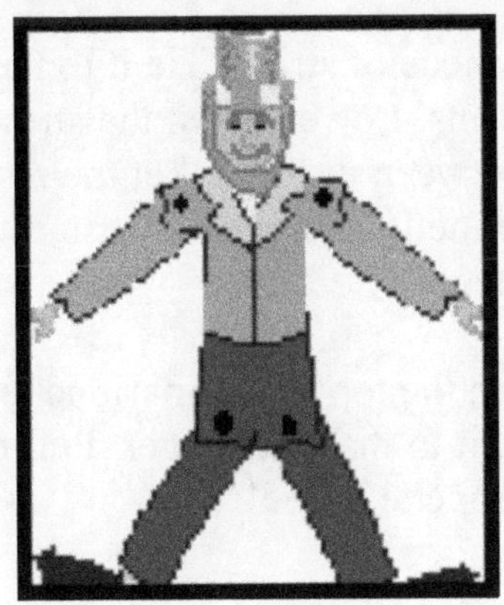

Materials

- Paper
- Glue
- Thin cardboard
- Scissors
- Hole punch
- 4 paper connectors
- String

Directions

1. Either draw a leprechaun on the paper or print one out from online. Cut it out and glue it to the cardboard.

2. Cut out the leprechaun from the cardboard. Cut off the arms and legs. Reattach the arms and legs with the paper connectors.

3. Take the needle and thread and punch a hole on the outer edge of each shoulder. Tie the string from one arm to another so it is taut.

4. Repeat step 3 on the legs, with the string connecting from the top of one leg to the other.

5. Take another piece of string. Tie it to the middle of the string between the arms. Lower down the string, tie it to the middle of the piece between the legs. Let the rest of the string dangle from the marionette. This is the string you will pull to move the arms and legs.

6. Punch a hole in the top of the marionette's head, and loop the string through it to make a hanger. Pull the dangling string to make the marionette dance!

81. Paper Dreidel

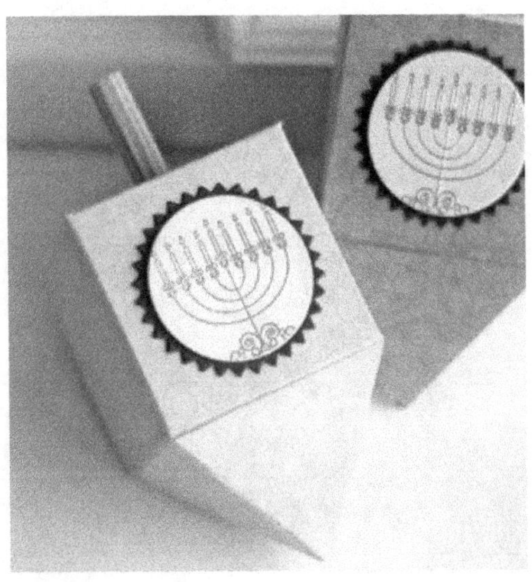

Materials

- Printer and paper
- Scissors
- Glue
- Crayons or markers
- A straw or short wooden dowel
- Thin cardboard (optional)

Directions

1. Find a dreidel template online. There are lots to choose from. Print it out. If you choose, you can glue the dreidel template to the cardboard. This will make the dreidel sturdier, but it will be more difficult to cut out.

2. Cut out the dreidel template. Decorate the dreidel however you'd like. Fold along the lines, and glue the dreidel together.

3. Push the straw or wooden dowel through the top to the bottom. This will allow you to spin the dreidel and play with your friends.

82. Metal Ornaments

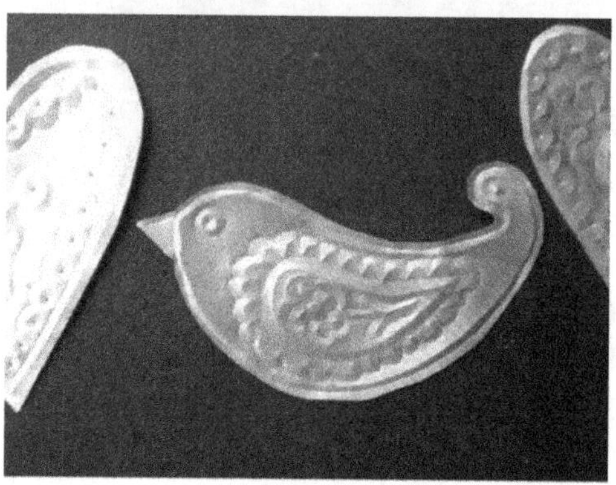

Materials

- Disposable pie plate or roasting pan
- Scissors
- Large nail
- String or yarn
- Scrap cardboard or newspaper

Directions

1. Work on the cardboard or a thick pile of newspaper to protect your workspace. Draw simple designs on the pie plate or roasting pan. Some ideas are a star, a crescent moon, a heart, or a bird.

2. Cut out the designs. Use the nail to make indents around the ornaments for decoration. Punch a large hole at the top of each ornament to tie the string. Loop the string or yarn through each ornament, and tie it together to create a hanger. Hang your ornaments on the tree!

83. Bird in A Birdcage

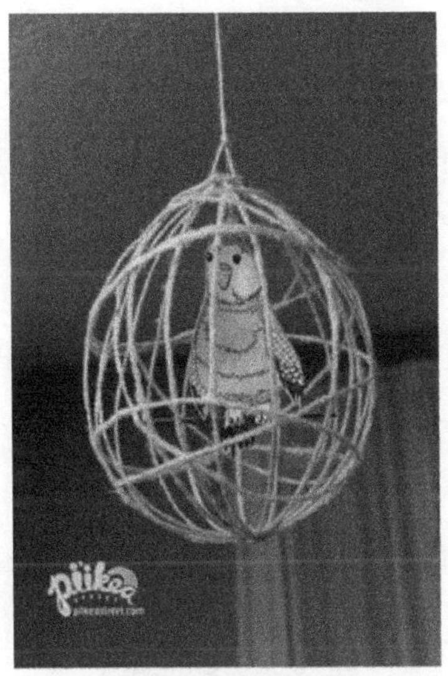

Materials

- Large balloon
- Construction paper
- String
- Flour and water
- Bowl
- Paintbrush
- Scissors

Directions

1. Mix ¼ cup flour with 1 cup of water. Have an adult bring the water to a boil, and then let it simmer for 3 minutes.

2. Remove from the heat, and allow the glue to cool. Blow up the balloon and tie it. Dip the string in the flour glue and wrap it around the balloon in all directions until it looks like a birdcage.

3. Once the glue has fully dried (it can take a couple of days), pop the balloon and remove it from the cage. Tie a piece of string to the top of the cage to hang it. Draw a bird on the construction paper.

4. Tie a little string to the top of the bird, and lower it into the cage. You will probably need to roll the bird up to get it into the cage. Now you have a paper bird in a cage.

84. Moon Rock Paint

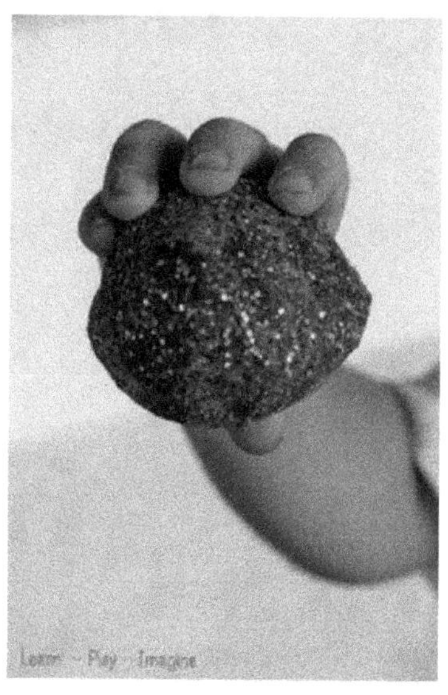

Materials

- Dark glitter
- Gray paint
- White chalk (4-5 pieces)
- Black construction paper
- Paintbrush
- Spoon
- Bowl

Directions

1. Crush the chalk into powder. In the bowl, mix the glitter and crushed chalk. You should add about the same amount of glitter as chalk.

2. Add a little water and gray paint. Stir it with a spoon until it is blended but a little chunky. Paint the mixture on brown paper. Don't brush out the clumps. This is what the surface of the moon looks like.

85. Homemade Lantern

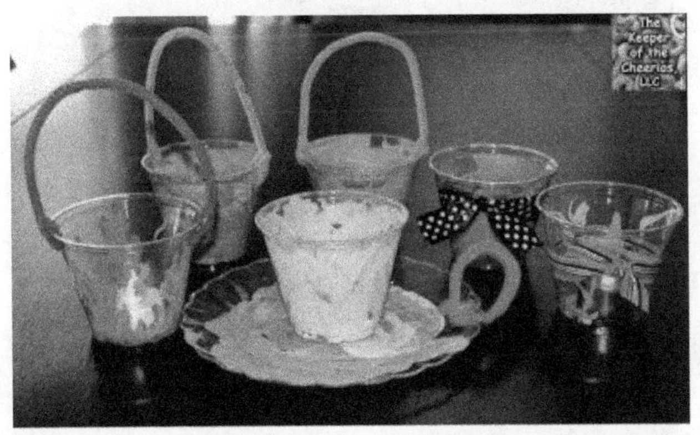

Materials

- Plastic cup
- Permanent markers
- Hole punch
- Twine or yarn
- Battery votive candle

Directions

1. Draw fun designs all over the cup with the markers. Punch holes on opposite sides of the top of the cup.

2. Tie a piece of twine or yarn from one side to the other to create a handle. Place the battery candle inside the cup. Now you have a lantern!

86. Pipe Cleaner Finger Puppet

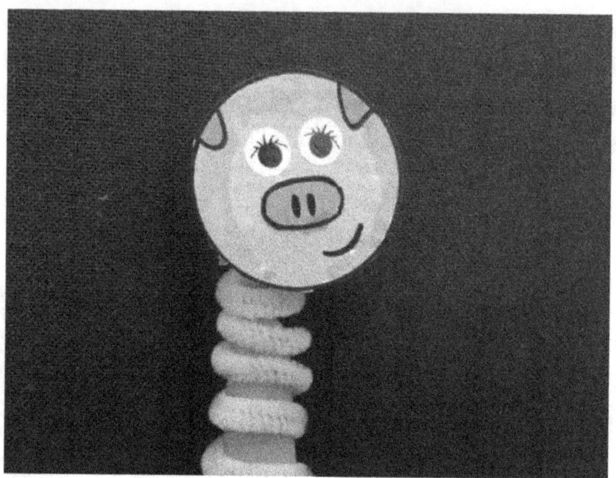

Materials

- Pipe cleaner
- Construction paper
- Markers
- Glue
- Scissors

Directions

1. Cut out a circle from the construction paper. It should be about 1" across. Draw a face on the circle with markers. It can be a person, animal, alien, or whatever you want.

2. Glue the end of the pipe cleaner to the back of the head. Allow the glue to dry completely. Wrap the pipe cleaner around your finger. Now you have a finger puppet!

87. Paper Plate Frisbee

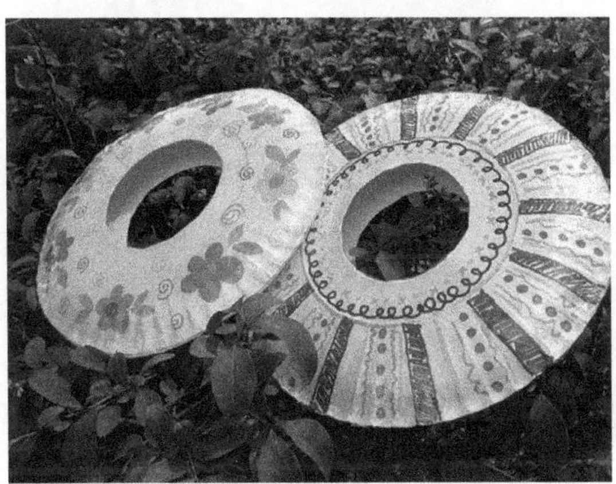

Materials

- 2 paper plates
- Hot glue and glue gun
- Paint and paintbrush
- Scissors

Directions

1. Paint the two paper plates whatever color you'd like. Allow the paint to fully dry. Once the plates are dry, cut a circle out of the center of each plate.

2. Hot glue the plates together to form a disc. The curved sides should face out. You are now able to throw the disc around with your friends!

88. Lava Lamp

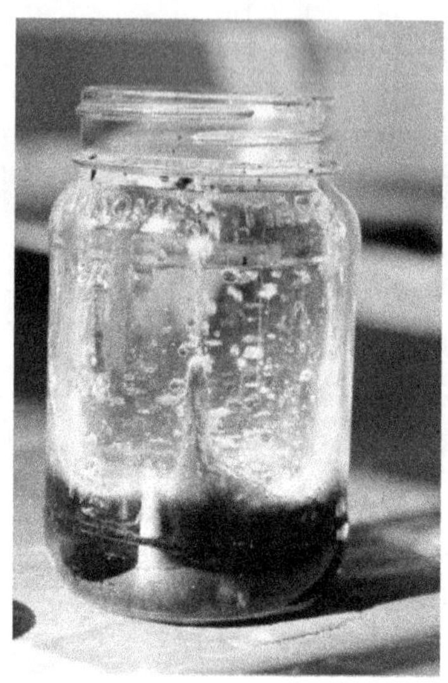

Materials

- Empty jar
- Alka-Seltzer tablets
- Water
- Cooking oil
- Food coloring
- A spoon

Directions

1. Fill the jar about 1/3 full of water. Add a few drops of food coloring and stir. Add cooking oil until you have almost filled the jar. Allow the oil to settle on top of the water for a couple of minutes.

2. Break the alka-seltzer tablet into four pieces, and drop them, one at a time, into the water. Watch what happens!

89. Flower Magnet

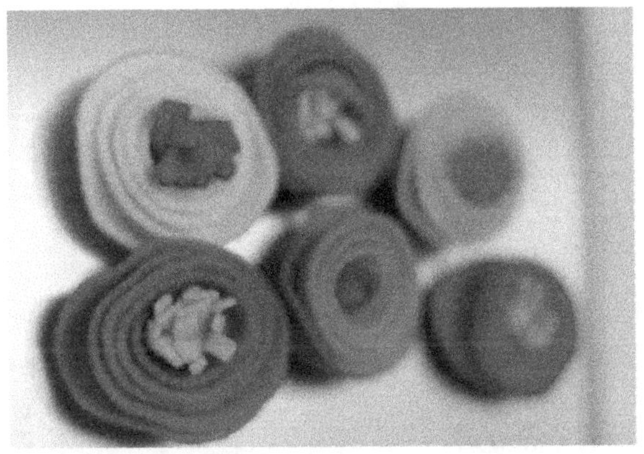

Materials

- Felt
- Scissors
- Strong magnet
- Thin cardboard circle
- Hot glue gun and glue

Directions

1. Cut the felt into a circle that is about 3" in diameter. Starting at the outside, cut a spiral into the center of the circle. Swirl the spiral into a rose shape by tightening it until it looks how you want it to look. Secure it with a bit of hot glue.

2. Glue a small piece of circular cardboard to the back of the rose. Hot glue the magnet to the cardboard. Fringe a small rectangle of felt. Spin it into a circle, and glue it inside the rose. Secure your rose to the fridge.

90. Paper Bead Necklace

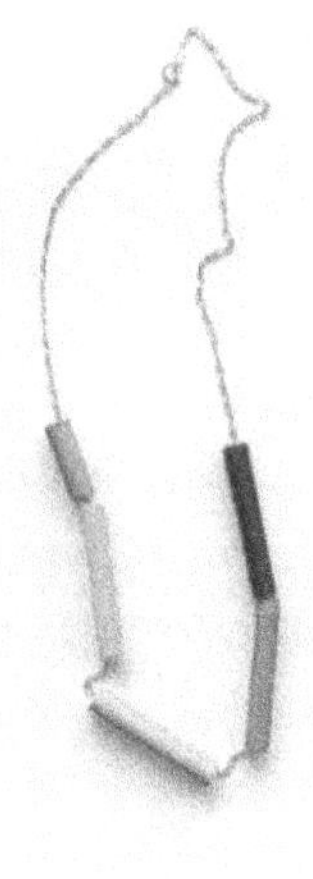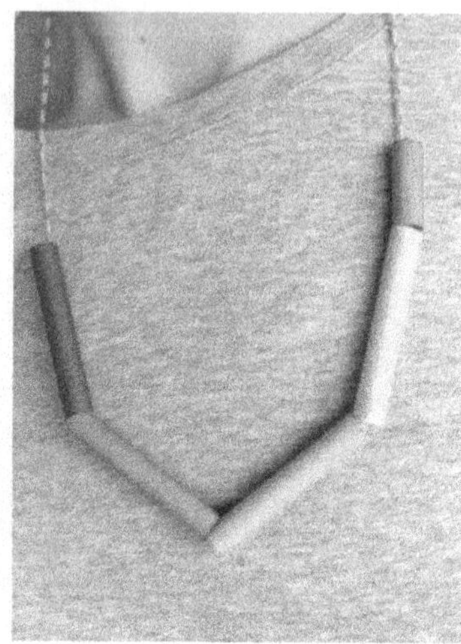

Materials

- Several different colors of cardstock
- Scissors
- Chunky knitting needle or dowel
- Paintbrush
- Mod-Podge
- Yarn

Directions

1. Cut the cardstock into several narrow triangular strips. Starting at the wider end, roll the paper into your knitting needle.

2. Cover the paper with a thin coat of Mod-Podge. Slip the bead off the needle and let it dry. Create as many beads as you'd like. String the beads onto the yarn into a necklace. Tie the ends together.

91. Cardboard Ring

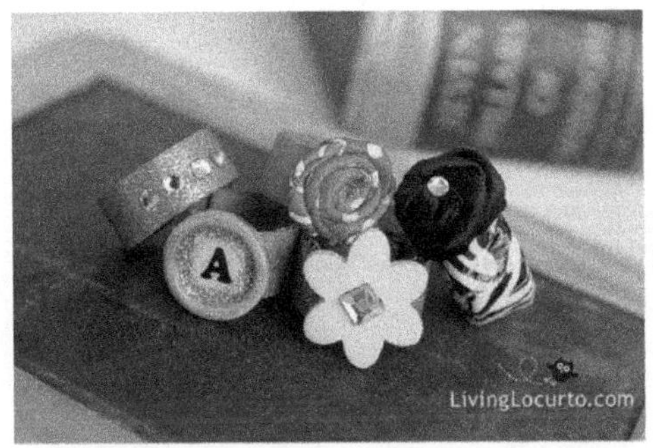

Materials

- Cereal box or other thin cardboard
- Scissors
- Marker
- Hot glue gun and glue
- Paint and paintbrush

Directions

1. Draw your favorite shapes on the cardboard. Cut out the shapes along with thin strips of cardboard to make the rings.

2. Wrap the ring around your finger, and have an adult hot glue the ring in place. Trim off any excess. Paint the shape cutouts, and hot glue them to the rings.

92. Car Tracks Wrapping Paper

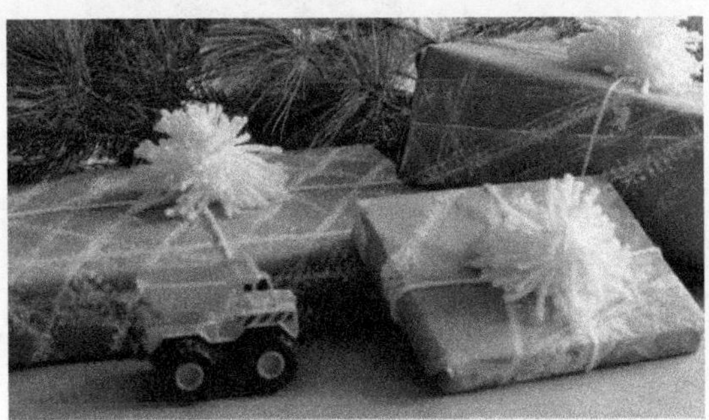

Materials

- Brown craft paper
- Paint
- A shallow container (like a plastic plate)
- Toy car
- Scissors

Directions

1. Roll out the craft paper and cut out a large piece. Pour some paint in the shallow container, and smear it around a bit with your fingers. Roll the wheels of the toy car through the paint.

2. Run the car over the craft paper forming car tracks all over it. Set the paper aside to dry. Use the paper to wrap your presents.

93. Citrus Peel Garland

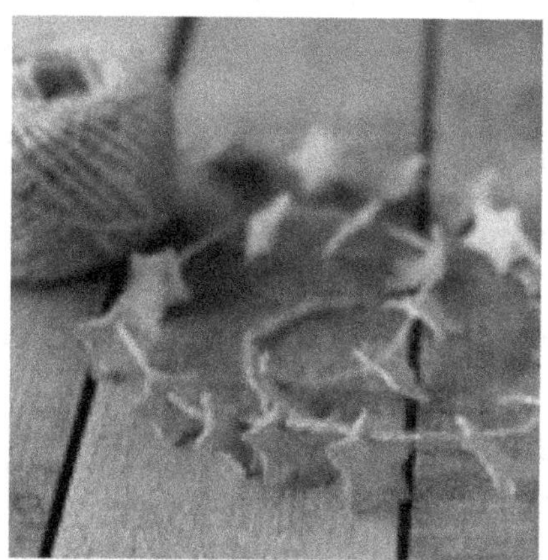

Materials

- Oranges
- A knife
- Scissors

- Baker's twine
- Cookie sheet
- Hand juicer
- Spoon
- Thumbtack

Directions

1. Have an adult cut the oranges in half. Juice the oranges with a hand juicer. Save the juice to drink later (or drink it now). Scrape the inside of the oranges clean with a spoon. Flatten the orange peels out and cut them into geometric shapes like stars, rectangles, or squares. Place the orange peels on a cookie sheet.

2. Have an adult put the cookie sheet in the oven at 200 degrees Fahrenheit for 1 ½-2 hours. Have an adult pierce each piece with a thumbtack. String the twine through the pieces and hang the garland in your home!

94. Monster Claws

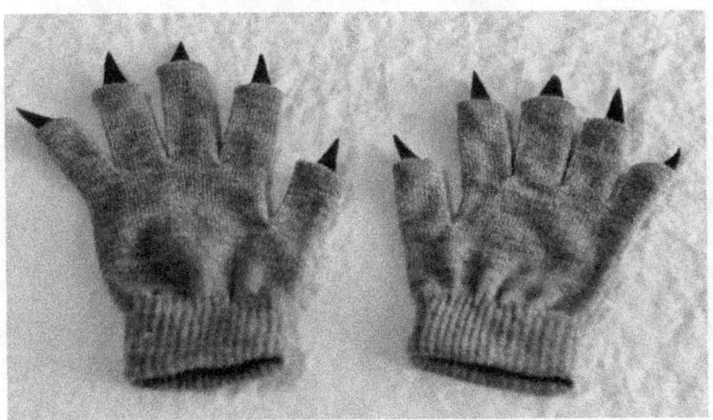

Materials

- Felt
- Scissors

- Hot glue gun and glue
- Knit gloves

Directions

1. Cut out ten tiny triangles from the felt. The base of the triangles should be the width of the fingers of the gloves. Tuck the base of each triangle into the tip of each finger, just a bit.

2. Hot glue the tips onto the ends of the fingers. Wear your gloves on Halloween or any other time you want claws!

95. Watercolor Resist Spider Web

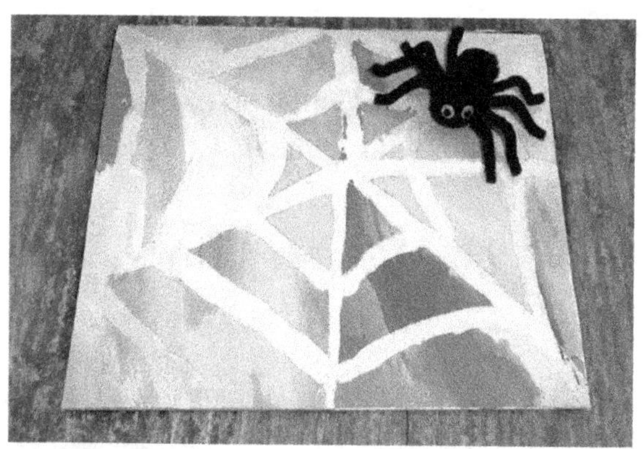

Materials

- Rubber cement
- Watercolor paper
- Watercolors and brushes
- Black pompom balls
- Scissors
- Hot glue and glue gun
- Googly eyes
- Black pipe cleaners

Directions

1. Draw a spider web with the rubber cement on the watercolor paper. Let it dry for a few hours. Paint over the spider web outlines so the whole paper is covered except for the places the cement covers.

2. Once everything is dry, peel away the rubber cement to see the spider web.

3. To make the spider, cut the pipe cleaners, and bend them to form eight legs. Glue the pompom balls to the pipe cleaner, and add the googly eyes. Glue the spider onto the web wherever you want.

96. Volcano in A Jar

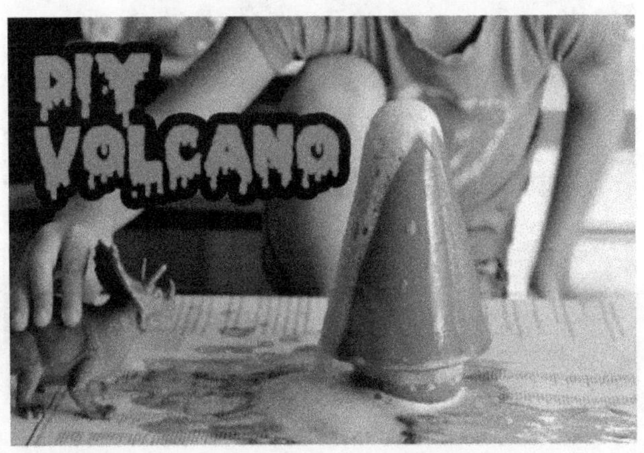

Materials

- 2 tablespoons baking soda
- ½ teaspoon salt
- Dish liquid
- Orange food coloring
- Vinegar
- Scissors

- Party hat
- Small glass jar

Directions

1. Take a party hat and cut the tip off. Cut zig-zags in the top with scissors. In a jar about the same height, or a bit shorter than the hat, add the baking soda, salt, and food coloring. Mix it well.

2. Add 1-2 squirts of dish liquid. Put the party hat on top of the jar. Pour the vinegar through the hole in the hat and into the jar. Watch the volcano erupt!

97. Sticky Window Art

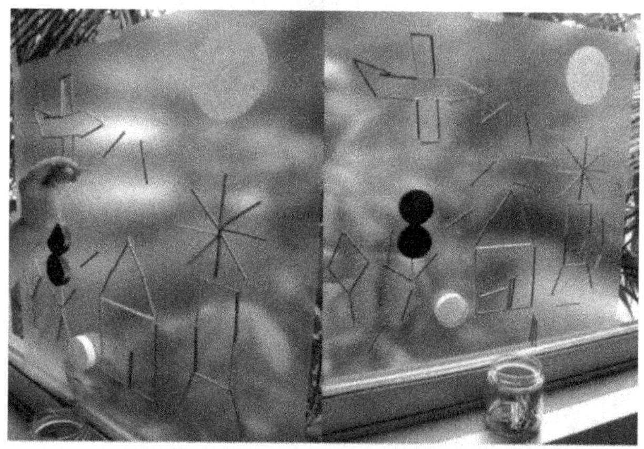

Materials

- Contact paper
- Scissors
- Sticky tape
- A window
- Anything small that you want to decorate with (toothpicks, bottle caps, cupcake liners, etc.)

Directions

1. Cut a large square of contact paper. Tape it to the inside of your window with the sticky side facing out.

2. Put tape on each corner and down the sides so it won't move or bunch up when you put things on or take them off. Press your small items into the contact paper in fun designs. Experiment with new patterns and shapes.

98. Homemade Quicksand

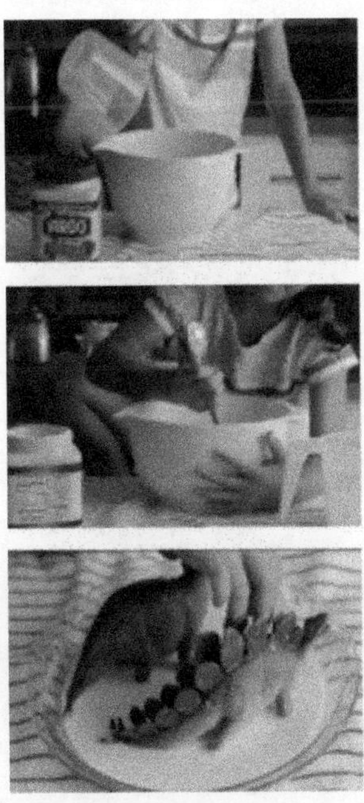

Materials

- Mixing bowl and spoon
- Shallow container (Tupperware works well)
- ¾ cup of water
- 1 cup cornstarch
- Yellow food coloring

Directions

1. Pour ¾ cup water into a bowl. Add 1 cup of cornstarch to the water. Add some yellow food coloring to make it look like sand. Stir the mixture together for about 5 minutes until it thickens.

2. Pour the mixture into a shallow container. Sink your hands or small toys into the "quicksand."

99. Plastic Cup Lighthouse

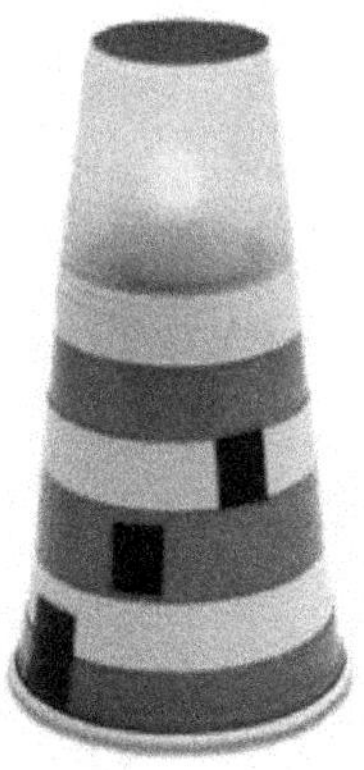

Materials

- Red plastic cup
- Smaller clear cup
- Battery operated tea light
- Scissors
- Black paper
- White tape
- Glue stick

Directions

1. Place the red cup upside down. Use the white tape to make two parallel stripes on the cup. Cut a door shape and two

windows out of the black paper, and glue them onto the lighthouse wherever you want.

2. Turn on the tea light, and place it on top of the lighthouse (the bottom of the cup). Place the smaller clear cup on top of the tea light.

Conclusion

This brilliant mix of 99 crafts for kids will teach you how to make things you can use and gifts that you and others will cherish.

The projects are educational and challenging for kids of all ages. But most importantly, they are fun!

Having tried the projects, kids will be inspired to get even more creative.

Last Chance to Get YOUR Bonus!

FOR A LIMITED TIME ONLY – Get my best-selling book "DIY Crafts: The 100 Most Popular Crafts & Projects That Make Your Life Easier" absolutely FREE!

Readers who have downloaded the bonus book as well have seen the greatest changes in their crafting abilities and have expanded their repertoire of crafts – so it is *highly recommended* to get this bonus book today!

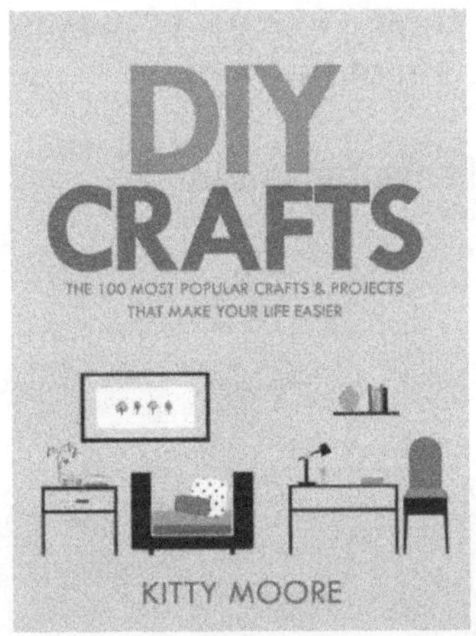

Get your free copy at:

ArtsCraftsAndMore.com/Bonus

Final Words

Thank you for downloading this book!

I really hope that you have been inspired to create your own projects and that you will have a lot of fun crafting.

I do hope that you and your family have found lots of ways to fill lazy afternoons or rainy days in a more fun way.

If you have enjoyed this book and would like to share your positive thoughts, could you please take 30 seconds of your time to go back and give me a review on my Amazon book page!

I really appreciate these reviews because I like to know what people have thought about the book.

Again, thank you and have fun crafting!

Disclaimer

No Warranties: The authors and publishers don't guarantee or warrant the quality, accuracy, completeness, timeliness, appropriateness or suitability of the information in this book, or of any product or services referenced by this site.

The information in this site is provided on an "as is" basis and the authors and publishers make no representations or warranties of any kind with respect to this information. This site may contain inaccuracies, typographical errors, or other errors.

Liability Disclaimer: The publishers, authors, and other parties involved in the creation, production, provision of information, or delivery of this site specifically disclaim any responsibility, and shall not be held liable for any damages, claims, injuries, losses, liabilities, costs, or obligations including any direct, indirect, special, incidental, or consequences damages (collectively known as "Damages") whatsoever and howsoever caused, arising out of, or in connection with the use or misuse of the site and the information contained within it, whether such Damages arise in contract, tort, negligence, equity, statute law, or by way of other legal theory.